THE
MIDDLE
NOTEBOOKES

Nathanaël

THE
MIDDLE
NOTEBOOKES

NIGHTBOAT BOOKS
New York

Falsehoods of Traversal

It is possible to say of the three *Notebookes* collected here, that they signal three different times, that their consonance is in a time that is theirs alone, in that they are *resonant* with each of these; what I once proposed translationally to a good friend as *concordant time signatures*. Put to the test of their synchronism, they might, in an imagined sense, pull apart the age to which they appertain, each having been unwittingly regulated by constraints that were initially foreign to it.

The Middle Notebookes began in French, as three carnets, written in keeping with three stages of an illness they knew nothing about: an onset and remission, a recurrence and further recurrence, a death and the after of that death. But this only became evident subsequently; the malady identified by these texts was initially a literary one, fastened to a body whose concealment had become, not only untenable, but perhaps, in a sense, murderous. It is possible, then, that more than anything, these *Notebookes* attest both to the commitment, and the eventual, though unlikely, prevention of, *a murder*.

But a book, one especially that is attached so irremediably to its present, is, perhaps of necessity, a *Selbstmörd*—a self-murder—in keeping with Ingeborg Bachmann's indictment of the present (*Heute*) in *Malina*. I can affirm that to use language is to commit the crimes which she has identified there and in *Der Fall Franza*, and which I've attended to somewhat in *Sisphyus, Outdone.* as elsewhere (*Asclepias*), but I could not have made better demonstration of this than through the kind of deliberation put into practice by these untimely carnets.

What I present here then, in English, is very much out of time. The three French carnets span three precise periods. *Carnet de désaccords*, June 2007–June 2008; *Carnet de délibérations*, August 2008–August 2009; and *Carnet de somme*, November 2010–November 2011. *The Middle Notebookes*, such as they are constituted here, now, combine in a single volume, a process extended past the writing of the carnets to their time of translation, spanning the latter half of 2010 and the first half of 2011: the time of thereafter.

To say that translation is a mode of falsehood is to say nothing new. In this sense, these *Notebookes* are no exception. What the English proposes to itself, and to its author, is a task of concordance,* an attempt at synchronising a body with a place, in a language that remains foreign to it. It takes the discordances, the deliberations, and the sum of the three years and realigns them with a present which may yet cease

---

*A word on concordance: my first thought was that the book could only write itself on the site of its own disaster—a place assigned as my birth place and in which I had never lived (never is misleading: I lived in Montréal for just under a year from 2003 to 2004; this is almost never, which is perhaps as close as one can hope to get once one has irreme-diably been assigned to a birth in a place). This decision was arrived at in error, and carried out in error, against a squall of painful, though instructive, discordances, an experience I might describe as being psychi-cally shrapnelled. The 850 mile drive from a dwelling numbered 5684 in

to be a present of exclusion, a fourth year, unaccounted for, and coincident with the end of a painter's last age.

In order to accomplish this, it employs various pretenses as arguments in favour of itself even as it recognises that its foundational impulse is destructive. The restive forces of language act against it, and the body that supplies the narratives therein is already convinced of its *de facto* non-existence. From out of these elements, the fragile belief that the constitution of these nothings may amount at very least to the suggestion of itself. This remains to be seen.

Through the process of translating these texts and then deciding several times, after having decided against doing so, to publish them as a book, I have admittedly had some fear of provoking a resonance disaster, something like the psychic equivalent of the initial failure of the Tacoma Narrows Bridge in November 1940; wherein the synchronic combination of this body (*mine*) in this language (*English*) in this city (*Chicago*) might exacerbate their frequencies, causing a significant catastrophe. Against this fear, I have decided to risk it along with everything else.

---

the Rosemont neighbourhood of Montréal just north of the fenced-in rail line to a provisional third-storey flat behind a door numbered 1348½ on Chicago's north side, aided in the process of correcting that misthought. Chicago is not without its disasters, and the duration of dwelling is long and not without disturbance; it is, however, a place in which, against every other place that has attempted to claim me nationally (France, Canada, Québec, each with their own objectionable particulars), it has been possible to imagine a place from which to speak. In other words a body that is not in a permanent posture of imminent departure.

...

The first part presented here, which exists in French as *Carnet de désaccords*, or Notebook of Discord, offers a particular set of difficulties which may benefit from some elucidation. This carnet developed in part out of the frustration of an abandoned manuscript, having become unwritable. One of the primary falsehoods, then, of the translation of this first part, is the presentation in English of passages from that manuscript, as though it had ever existed in English at all. It hadn't, and so the notebook's complaint—addressing the unwritten, unwritable book—is in a sense an imagined complaint—imagined, largely because for the majority of my writing life, I have kept English and French distinct from one another, as of two separate selves that refused to speak to each other. Part of this work of translation is meant to suture something of that tear, without adhering to anything resembling a notion of perfectibility; simply the breaches, here, are permitted to be visible, and this defect of antecedence is one of them—there is no abandoned manuscript in English. It is re-invented here, for the sake of the *Notebookes*. I enjoy this subterfuge, and don't believe it to rob Part I (Discord) of its principal disagreement with the question of consolation. It remains inconsolable, just as Part II (Deliberation) remains unliberated, and Part III (Summation), the object of its own summary execution.

The treatment of passages quoted from French works in this text is very much out of character with other books I've published, in which the French has disrupted the legibility of the English, divesting it at least to some degree of its priority. In *The Middle Notebookes* and thus far exceptionally, the majority of passages from French works are presented in an English translation, sometimes mine, sometimes an existing translation, perhaps modified. In instances where no translation is provided, this is in keeping with the demands made by the work at a given time. The French sources can be consulted at the back of this volume. Other languages are seldom tampered with. The bibliographies provided are offered as summaries of each part. They are not exhaustive, but they do provide a suggestion of books that were near me during the time of writing, some of which I actually read. Where there are divergences between the French carnets and the English notebookes, they are deliberate. Let the adventurous reader uncover them. And foremost, let these *Middle Notebookes* have their own flawed life in this English to which they are now spuriously assigned. They have nothing more to say to the carnets, which mercifully abandoned them at the border. Whatever else I may have overlooked will be attended to by the *Notebookes* themselves; and if it is not, then it is deserving of that oblivion.[*]

—Nathanaël
Chicago, June 2011

---

[*] There is the question, also, of the letter "e" which I have left unaddressed. If pressed, I might say that it is the unpronounced part of me.

The Middle Notebookes

To John Beer
&
To Judith Goldman

for inestimable auspices
and secondment

...

To Rachel Gontijo Araújo

OS SENTIMENTOS *vastos não têm nome*.
(Hilda Hilst)

...

these Middle Notebookes
of traversal

in the after of their time.

(2007–2010;
2010–2011)

DISCORD
(Consolation)

Often I don't want to listen and often I can't look. Like when I couldn't bear the sight of the dying horse which had fallen off the cliff at Hermagor, for whose sake I walked for miles to fetch help, but I left it behind with the shepherd boy who couldn't do anything either, or the time I couldn't stand the sound of Mozart's C-Minor Mass or the gunshots in a village during Carnival. // I don't want to talk, it all upsets me, in my remembering.

—*Ingeborg Bachmann*

It all dried out little by little. It became thin as a leaf, thin and transparent like a very fine blade of glass; transparent, then it broke without a sound, it disappeared.

—*Eugène Ionesco*

The present solicits its consolations.

This: That it might be possible, (for me), to write the book of a kind of consolation. Think nothing of it. The book has carried me, carried me out, with little regard for the consequences. Now that this effort has exhausted itself, now that language has spoken me to the point of exhaustion, "now I prefer the garden to the quotidian. I prefer our letters to 'writing.' I prefer languor to light. The cats to speaking. The city has become unbearable. Nor the form of the body." I have incited doubt. Doubted in everything.

...

Though letters, even displaced letters, pulse with the tremor that is the purview of the body—the thing—cast off in favour of the current. Torn to shreds, burned, read and reread, forgotten or lost, they remain fastened to the wind, ardently encircling the poor limits imposed on this feeble existence. *Poor* for having believed in it. *Feeble* for not having believed enough.

...

And yet it must only be possible for consolation to be put to the test at the very moment of a death or a disappearance. In such a case, the gesture of consolation will have no conduit, and turn from the place of its execution, against the body that would submit it to another body whose disappearance rejects it with violence, for its inability to receive. Or else, its reception cannot be verified. From that moment forward, consolation is no longer consolation, but pettiness, despair, exploitation.

...

When I hold in my arms the disappearing body, not dead, not living, held back by my determination, my refusal, my stubbornness. When this fragile packet of flesh and bones gathers against me and I integrate it. When I sleep without shaking, balanced at the edge of the bed, stalking gasps. When the door opens onto the garden at four a.m. and I know that I need only walk to the other end, I am always already done for. If I step out, I am done for. If I cry out or shake, the integrated body hasn't the courage to die of itself. I stalk death, I disavow it. I integrate it. I integrate all the disappearing bodies.

...

Two winters in a row I fall on the stairs leading from the porch to the garden. The first time, my arms are full. The second time, they are empty. I don't bother with this distinction. The body that struck the cement wasn't mine. I picked it up, I carried it. There was nowhere to go. Outside, inside, the wall separating the living room from the porch could just as easily have been a torn skin. It was exactly this. The tear worsened with the advancing season. The hip became detached and the small knot that formed there in permanence is henceforth under foreign occupation. It's all very well that I am the foreigner in question, I have repatriated all of my sad bodies there.

...

My mother has only one brother whom she can trust. He died before she was born. As for me, I would not say no to a dead brother. The space of compromise would be considerably enlarged. Attempts have already been made to convince me that it is not good to dance on the bellies of the dead. Fair enough, as long as the ontological distinction between the living and the dead is dispensed with. Death is not an exoneration and it would do well to guard from being socially moralising. We might heed these words of Benjamin's rather than espouse a pious attitude toward that which was insupportable at the outset of its coming to mortality: "Only the historian is firmly convinced that even the dead will not be safe from the enemy if he wins. And this enemy has not ceased to be victorious." Here, the enemy could just as easily take the form of a dead relative, persistently exhumed.

Claude is born. There is no doubt. Claude is born on the roof of a house amid birds. Beneath a marauding sky. The year of the disappearances. The year of the effluvial deaths. And the railway cabals. The year the birds flew off for good. With small flags of flesh in their beaks.

...

Why bother distinguishing between dreams and nightmares. One is clearly but one aspect of the other. If it were necessary to submit to some evidence, statistically, the latter would far overtake the former. I prefer to leave aside this sort of distinction. But, since the subject is before me, these days I have noticed that the entrapment characteristic of most of my dreams has been replaced by a vertiginous verticality. The airs are steadfastly imposing themselves, occupying the space hitherto reserved by my subconscious for labyrinthine, but terrestrial, perambulations. By which I mean against, or even underneath, the earth. The dimension of the dream cannot be measured. It isn't absolute. That I may often be incapable of recognising a dream for what it is— but what is it?—leads me to a troubling question, tied to the paralysis provoked by dreaming. Provocation seems to bear some relationship to movement that is abrupt, sometimes even brutal; paralysis to a desire for movement, to movement enclosed in the body that believes itself to be capable of movement, but is unable to accomplish a single gesture, even the most "automatic" of gestures, *breathing*. The lungs are arrested by the weight of immobility. If, then, the dream is situated somewhere between what calls itself a body and what does not call itself a body, but is nonetheless a constitutive, even contingent, part of it—might it not be equally just to presume that it is capable of *provoking* movement? The question I have been asking myself for a week is this: is it possible to commit suicide while sleeping? These thoughts are far from Camus, but was not "his" country suicided by a dream?

...

Ever since I learned, sitting between the two speakers placed discreetly on my work table, connecting me to the world, that the word *Birkenau* meant "little birch prairie," the small bit of confidence I still maintained in relation to translation, the bit of hope I poured into that ontological, even revolutionary, task, has resolutely vanished. The voice of filmmaker Marceline Loridan-Ivens has convinced me, without making a single argument, without even the slightest involuntary nod or gesticulation. I knew the breath of language to be contaminated, but the lure has taken the form of a white hole, dazzling and strangely unsupportable.

...

If I catch fire in my bed at twelve, I must not be paying attention. The dream of the ten following years confirms this in the form of a seal on the inside of my body. A single giant hand that covers my entire face. After, the bodies come one after another to accomplish their task.

...

An eighteen-year-old woman sleeps with a fifty-year-old man. The scandal provoked by this audacity is immediately corrected in 1962 as in 1997. The woman's older brother assumes his role by travelling the seven hundred kilometres which separate him from his sister to give her a beating. Thirty years later, the same woman, who is no longer eighteen, calls upon the same brother, who must be close to seventy, to correct her own daughter in a similar fashion. The daughter is twenty-six. I come to wonder how it is in this case—which is far more common than one might like to admit—one might justify the concept of succession, swoon before the notion of lineage, adhere to a cult of *blood*. The woman is the brother's accomplice. She falls back (even unconsciously) on her own experience—her history—in order to convince herself of the justness of this barbarity. Thus does one arrive at an exposition of protectionism, i.e. whose interests are protected by such acts of violence. There is always profit to be gained. These are commonly referred to as family matters. So be it. The dam has burst. History is before us. The deluge itself.

Genealogy is cum-stained and riddled with "corrections." There's nothing to do besides hang from the family tree. Or else cut it down.

...

I hold in my hand a pine cone collected the day before my departure from Toronto. It vibrates with a truth of its very own, that of the witness who does not intend to be a witness. I pick it up near a bridge I am obliged to cross on all fours. I cross it several times, slowly, deliberately. I am after something which no longer bears any relation to the bridge. I am very aware of my ridicule. And then I am not thinking about it anymore, I am elsewhere. I waited three years to cross this bridge. It took all this time to condition myself not to straddle the guard-rail. My dreams instruct me as to the value of the cry and the fall, neither of which are mine. It wasn't a matter of freefalling toward the ground, but of bringing back a body. Of leaning into the cry released at the moment the hands loosened their hold and the air left the lungs. Of allowing myself to catch in the last breath. There was the determined march from the house to the bridge. There was the straddling of the guard-rail. And the release. Then... I hesitate in the space between. That's where I begin the collection of a new lexicon. A lexicon of an impossible probability, that of prevention. Thus: guard-rail, parapet, banister, hand-rail, balustrade. I am not the only one going off the rails. I note, as soon as my mouth becomes encrusted with the vocabulary of bridges and balconies, that the edge of the road, like the sea, is a limit demarcation. By that I mean not that it limits the body —a body of water or earth—but that the body learns a limit situation, the urgency of the call.

...

We learn nothing from buildings by limiting ourselves to a study of their facades—their doors, windows, and walls. Their frameworks (wood, metal, vinyl) and their coverage (stucco, aluminium, brick, stone, or plaster). Openings and coverings. Transparency and subterfuge. Closure and bravado. During my first visit to Chicago, buildings presented themselves to me otherwise; they offered me a new sense, an unexpected form of approach. By their rooftops. That is something worth considering. Having lived in cities which privilege underground public transit, I wasn't expecting my vision of a city to be overthrown by the simple fact of an elevated rail that follows its centenarian course at the same height as, and sometimes above, the buildings of residential neighbourhoods. Thus is exposed the most intimate aspect of a building: its covering.

...

Mallarmé is instructive in that he demonstrates that the body rots—decomposes—at the same rate as writing.

...

Consolation participates of a space that is complicit with force. The dejection of centuries is the same categorical dejection of the species. This assertion is not verifiable without recourse to Simone Weil. What she designated by the term *décréation* was the culmination in a single body of the force of force. An ardour. A fatal zeal. If she refused to eat, it was also perhaps for having been overfull of world.

...

When we meet, it is clear that desire has anticipated us. You lie down, I remain standing, undecided. Now I am him. He renders possible the I that I wanted for myself. The error was in not anticipating the collapse. The collapse of one at the edge of the other. The result of this precariousness is a capitulation expressed by the equation: me + you = you. First, I dream of touch as something diaphanous, imprecise. It's the beginning. Then I dream you clamber over me like a mountain. You survey me like a secret. There is defeat. It rushes at us without hesitation. The "we," here, is cause for confusion. There isn't: "we." There is one dispossessing the other.

...

Israel is of the order of disaster. The very particular disaster of nomination. The disaster is the inverse of the possible. It is the desire to *fix* the dream, to draw its boundaries.

...

If I claim that letters are of the order of a tremor, it's that I wish to be available to this sensation called *trembling*. Trembling is of the order of the unexpected, which respects no order. Disorder is in a sense its word order. The unexpected is not inexhaustible. It has no *telos* either. It follows from the seductive idea that the unexpected could not take place. Which means that it could just as easily take place. It is neither threshold, nor *limen*, nor even abyss. It is neither opening, nor breach, nor fissure. It doesn't serve to patch or to drain or to retain. It is always elsewhere, and as soon as it approaches, it has always already exhausted itself. Its exhaustion is what astounds. The fact of its passage and its immediate disappearance and the body transformed with neither support nor diction.

...

At a young age, after having read several books, I resolved to live a life absent of memory. It put me on a wrong track. Memory is not absent. Rather, it is blocked in the body where it only manifests as discomfort and dizziness, sometimes a very sharp pain, which is also unlocatable, there, between the scapula. One day, many years later, after having pored for some time over the problem of the burdened vacuity of my memory, my sister offered me my memory as a consolation. It wasn't because of her voyage to Morocco, nor her refusal to travel to France, but because of the very rudimentary problem of its organisation. Where, tell me, after all the space occupied by the absent memory, was I to put the fresh memory of so long ago? How was it to be distributed in the body? Now that I had it, I could no longer be rid of it, I couldn't hope for it anymore. The relief that came with this *knowledge* was mitigated by the sudden erasure of the question of my memory. My memory—which was not mine, but rather a graft—didn't tell me anything more than did its absence. It only succeeded in exhibiting my suffering otherwise.

...

When A. writes, "The present is locked, almost impossible," he doesn't know that I spent last night watching—not dreaming—enclosure and flight. Just as one watches over the dead, even an anticipated death. My question for him, then, is this: does memory belong to death? It seems this is what the newcomers to North America of the last four centuries intended to put into practice. Raze the past, which amounts to a cocktail of genocides smothered by imperialist discourses of the subsisting dominant powers.

Canada, for example, promotes its two miserable solitudes, but this myth of the schism is a simple renewal of the old struggle between France and England. Are we so resolutely duped, so stubbornly amnesic, as to not want to draw the connection between a cast-off past and the demonstrations which formulate a present of exclusion?

...

In Sofia, I have only one word on my tongue. It adhered to me as soon as I arrived: *zstoto*—"because." In Bulgaria, I was at all times in a posture of causality. I was making ties. In Ljubljana, however, it was supplication—*prosim*—"please" and "thank you," which situated me. I was at the mercy of my ignorance, and of the good deeds of a city which made a small place for me, with great generosity. In Euskadi, I never said farewell or good-bye, but *geroarté*—"see you later"— my mouth borrowing that familiarity, and propelling my body into the irresolute space of temporality. *Geroarté*, causality undone, supplication dismissed, I was free to move toward the unknown, to stake that freedom which drew the contours of a friendship that was ever postponed and never declined, of unwagered familiarity.

...

If, in order to console oneself of a book, as of a love, it were necessary to be rid of it, so be it. I had put myself in the way of writing a book *of a kind of consolation*. A book to distance me from prior books. But the weight of commitment smothered the reasoning I'd adopted in relation to this unwritten book. As in relation to an unlived life in which the awareness of having not lived prevents any form of living at all. To open it, I had adopted the following two lines: The thing. I would like to tell it to you very simply. The very articulation of this hoped-for simplicity immediately effaced itself, complicating the thing which was already complicated at the outset of its simplification. Where was I to take such a text? It is the promise of the book that tore the thing from me, on the one hand, and nailed it, on the other, irremediably, to all the books prior to it. Slowly I rid myself of it. For four years, I sat before it, rereading the several lines I'd consigned to it, and the more familiar they became, the more unbearably unavoidable. The book of opening, of a kind of lightness, which was to have consoled me of the other books, closed itself brutally against the body that was no longer capable of dislodging itself. I slid the fine blade of avowal beneath the membrane. The book was a voracity for death overturned.

...

Malraux: "Don't forget that the one who watches us, I mean history, which is judging and will judge us, calls for the sort of courage that goes in and wins, not the courage that consoles...."

This dialectic of courage distributed between gain and consolation neatly traces the figure of a vice—*history*—whose two jaws are pulverised as they draw shut.

...

To F., July 2, 2007: "Do you know that I am finally reading *L'espoir*? In it, I found a lottery ticket dated June 24, 1976, #19025340, series 72. I imagined the ticket was being used as a bookmark. But then I find this: on the last page, you keep a record of your tickets by drawing up a list in blue ink, in which the ticket and series numbers are duly inscribed:

June 24		
23053	serie	96
95740	serie	88
89225	"	44
71412	"	4
35298	"	65

The book will have served as a register; instead of the ticket holding your place while you are reading, the book occupied the place of this archive. Is that what hope is for you?"

...

Agamben: "Language (reason) is that whereby something exists rather (potius, more powerfully) than nothing."

Language is never consoling. It is the first instrument of Reason. The something that is in opposition to the nothing, barely thing, but thing enough for it to be made into a *raison d'être*. Ontological hyperbole. Drain.

...

This summer of 2007 I am tracking Antibes' forest fires, as one might track a scent, a lover, a memory. The bit of flesh still capable of recollecting that place from twenty years ago, burns with its incapacity to stop the ravaging fires, those earthly sores that make light of the landscape and its inhabitants. In the place of my memory, I have unbandageable, blistering hives, seeping rage and regret. This outbreak is of a piece with the thicketed lands whose aridity scores my arms, sickening me.

...

The child mother is lying in the sand. She hides her face in the crook of an arm. The mountain admonishes her. The neighbour falls to the ground. The roaring sea amid the gunfire.

...

A child born of first cousins is condemned to enclosure. She is neither daughter nor bastard. Neither orphan nor offspring. She is the fruit of a single parenthood, the slaked fruit of a unique antecedence that claims her completely. There is no share, there is absolute possession. She is a borderless territory, under constant surveillance and governance, a drainless nothing. Until the day she passes the part of the world said to be unique and unmarked (for there is no need for markings in an inexhaustible world, reiterated without modulation). She passes and bursts, the shards of her embed themselves in the multiple worlds she henceforth inhabits synchronically to signal the impossibility of realisation.

...

Each day begins with the anticipation of a call. A small note slid into the mail slot, a bird song cutting through the fence, a telephone ringing in the environs, are enough for the conversation of the day to begin. Thus does the outside attach itself to the inside, and become indistinguishable. The gate at Caluire closes onto the elevator of the Eighteenth Arrondissement. La Croix-Rousse or Marcadet-Poissonniers. A single same scent at the nostrils calls up a breeze, overburdens the body with crude irresolute sensations surfaced from a past that lies as to its indulgence.

...

If chance had imagined itself to be consoling (it opens

what appears to be closed and dematerialises that which imagines itself to be firm), it is immediately corrected by the inevitable. It is neither threshold nor enclosure, but the torn skin of an incapable wall. The contract with chance is intractable. One agrees to leave a part of oneself behind. Considered this way, chance is of the order of lack, of ravishment. But it is perhaps just as advantageous to take an approach other than this one, and to see in the casting off—however surprising and severe—provoked by chance, the fortuitous, and thus unexpected, encounter with that other part of the self that has remained concealed all this time due to a lack of attention. As soon as one leaves, is torn from, one's language, one learns to speak otherwise. Then is it no longer a matter of the echo, but of a lament occupying the space of absence. An incommensurable, expectant absence. This is one way of thinking the inevitable, which is also the unthinkable, and so always within reach. Within reach of the voice. And resolutely unapproachable.

...

The abandoned manuscript is decidedly not abandoning me. The corrective (this notebook) reinforces the futility of abandon. Abandon of being for being. I want to relinquish responsibility with regard to history, to be exonerated by it. Never mind. History keeps my word and my word keeps me. This time I will not overstep. Not the river nor the thin sidewalk separating me from the other body, the other body that runs into the one that won't go.

The abandoned manuscript reveals itself to be the letter of a slow retrieval. As raw material, I have at my disposal two dates: a birth in 1939; a death (murder, it is said) in 1946. July and July, Oran. I leaf through a memory that isn't mine in favour of a past that offers itself as an injury inflicted upon time. It is in fact *a tendency*, this desire that inhabits me like an injunction, to uproot a history that is by definition faulty. Because in my family, if one must resort to such language—the dead are—at times—more reliable than the living. Suppose this one is. This singular death that anticipated nearly all of us, and commands me ever since I learned of it. This death is lucid, and consequently the pain associated with it exceeds the pettiness of the whole insidious quotidian to arrive this far. The hands are arid and the cries are heard only by the wind. Just like the bird, we die in song. How do I answer no, from my own death?

...

Lévinas: "It is in the being that begins—not in its relations with its cause—that we find the paradox of a being that begins to be, or, of distinguishing, in this being, what takes on the weight [of being] from that weight itself."

Le port is an approximate assonance of *l'apport*. Must one see in this weight the share of an offering? An offering that has its share of pangs, carried *precariously*, with all the gravity, with all the deference due to torment. Thus, one's own approximation.

...

I implement a methodology of drainage. Not only because of my failing memory. But because I need to make room. In this sense, I am not engaging in accumulation and archiving—of knowledge, or objects, or of people—but in their removal. In this way, I facilitate their movement. It is quite likely that my indifference to chronology and causality is linked to a predilection for *moments*. A book would thus be a *moment* of writing. To arrive at the next book, it is necessary for the previous book to have left me. This is also true of the thoughts in this notebook. Not that one could not coexist with the other; all exist concurrently, but their superimposition, or their simultaneity, provokes in me a sometimes dizzying paralysis. I always begin from emptiness, but it is emptiness replete.

...

One of the consequences of having lived in so many places is that I am always in the process of leaving somewhere. It has taken me twenty years of displacement to arrive at this observation: with the first threshold crossed, I set off an inevitability of departures that it is impossible to undo. It is a multiple departure that will never be corrected by my installation in a single—even "definitive"—place. There is no one place. I may very well be watering the garden on Winchester Avenue, all the other gardens come mathematically to disturb my orientation. It is neither errance, nor indecision, but a problem of degrees and morcellation. Even in the simplest of equations, wherever I may be, I occupy the space of the fraction bar.

...

Graffiti in Barcelona (2004) : *Torero bueno* / *torero muerto*. In urgent washed out, almost illegible blue letters. And scribbled in thick, black, sinister letters above these words : **TORTURA**. I will never forgive Almodóvar the romanticised death of the toro in *Hable con ella*. I sleep at the foot of a city. I sleep and I wake and I fall asleep again. With one hand, I grope for the floor, with the other, the river's edge. This chassé-croisé puts me in my—infinite—place—and the book in its own, unwritten. One must die at the edge of a place in order to be able to traverse it. How else might one otherwise approach the exonerated share of one's displacements? And the slaughter that convoked them?

...

A person leaves a house, with a clock under one arm, returning later with a book. A person sitting in the shade (the city buckles this July under the pressure of suffocating heat) observes the coming and the going, and proposes out loud, not addressing anyone in particular, that time is worth at least the verb that conjugates it. And yet it is not a question of value, nor of weight, but of expectancy. The rains still don't come and the body hesitates—insists—between the passage and the voice.

...

In the city in which I live, I rent a room for a change of air. The window opens onto the rail line and the sound of the train disturbs my nights. I cross the park on the way home instead of walking past the shed. And under a bridge reeking of human piss instead of the dog piss of my neighbourhood. The bed serves as a desk and the desk as a kitchen and my first mistake is to set about howling on the cast iron balcony. One can make the body forget its trajectory, if only for a time, but the voice that leaves by the throat brings the whole city back to the beginning. And the voice beseeches: not again!

...

Boy or buoyed? How does one avoid choice in the midst of the choosing imposed by a language that always wants to *translate*, in other words to relegate. Claude Arnaud's *René* and the Claude of my (unwritten) text kiss one another on the mouth, embrace and imbricate themselves in the realisation of their indivisibility. They make love and they make much of it: the cinderblock, the building, the score. One is born on an Algerian mountain in 1938, the other in a spent mouth, undated. Regardless, they are exhausted by their ardour and their invisibility, and the contusioning embrace of a crustacean tongue.

...

By dint of my scarcely manifest thirty-seven years, I come to ask myself, along with Frédéric Ferney, and with insistence, whether there will be a mistral or not. The question, by all counts a fairly innocent one, possibly even ridiculous, and certainly distracting, and with a gap of several thousand kilometres (I am not in Avignon, and unless I am mistaken nor am I touring a performance), strangely sums up what proves to be the passage from *nothing* to *nothing*, in the sense that the *turn* I am rigorously anticipating is precisely characterised by its absence. Defenceless, I refer to the unmodulated terrain of this city, this *flatland*, where the articulation of the landscape is not as one might expect to find it. This unhilled city, with its domesticated swamp, its fortified lake and the inverted current of its river, razed then rebuilt after the great fire of 1871, is both of the order of immutability and the spectacular. What does it hold for me, beyond a conservatism enticed by hyperbolic masculinity? I raise my eyes to a sky that can only be residual, despite its colour, magnanimously engendered by the kerosene, and recall that *there is* frequents the *there is not* of my dreams. For me, then, nothing, and it is this nothing which I must cultivate, in the absence of the rupture that accommodates me to my unreality.

...

Édouard Glissant: "For writing, like the One, is a consensual lack."

...

To do and to undo. The disconcerted flow of language imitates the stutter of the body discouraged by its distance. Writing so as not to divulge, speaking so as not to say, touch so as not to engage, looking without seeing, pleasing or displeasing, is one and the same, some might say. But this *Un*—wishing itself unique—is the shattered one, the singular in pieces, scattered. "The pack of parched selves rushes at those morsels of meat." The starved and the fed, for whom the very idea of *hunger* is untenable, for it is thwarted by the discourse held against it. Peeled back, the skin reveals nothing other than the absurdity of the vented gaze. To the undertaking I respond with reversal and outpouring.

...

In my books, there are no *characters*, but rather *instants of being* or better yet presences. The character is already complicit in the lure of fiction. I have no interest in these entities, these totalities; not that I seek in or through writing a realism language will never be able to account for. Rather it is a matter of accounting for the fragmentary character of being, in perpetual displacement in relation to the self, which fiction has been incapable of because of its infallible adherence to a beginning and an end. My texts have already gone off their heads; and situate themselves in the multiple and unreconcilable trajectory of the outburst that occurs with the breach. It isn't even a matter of following the flow of liquid spurting from the body, but of the literal (and literary) pluralisation that takes place at the time of the dismemberment of the self. *A pack of selves* writes Glissant. I am listening to the anguished barking—or the desperate howls (Gide).

...

(No garden other than the one at the door. In the *même au même*, there is the infinitesimal adjustment, the small disturbance which is of the order of a whisper and not a breach. Abandon the evidence. Unfold.)

...

In this sense, character is complicit with consolation. It is not reliable. Claude is neither a character nor a human being. He might be *limbic*. Not altogether embodied, not entirely dissolved, but *disposed*. (Even dissolution suggests having-been). He is of history, for he has been so many times recounted. And, precisely for having been recounted, he is barely capable of existing. Like writing, he would be—"precisely this compromise between freedom and remembrance, (...) this freedom which remembers and is free only in the gesture of choice, but is no longer so in duration" (Barthes). His mountain is a specific mountain, his sea, a sea that carries a common name, and his war, an affliction that exceeds the boundaries that lay claim to it. But, as soon as he is *placed* somewhere, he flees. As soon as a *particular* voice adheres to his body, he is plunged into the mute marshes and floods, smothered.

The paradox is this: being in its particularity—by which I mean the anecdotal being—reduces the reach of the emergent text. In order to survive it, it is necessary not— or only scarcely—to resemble it, in order to be able to enter into language, to be at the *level* of language, whose first gesture will always be to fossilise (in sum, to provoke capitulatation); to escape language, he must become *echo*. For Claude to be written, he must cease to be situated atop É.'s shoulders. His death must fall from the hands of the Nazi-sympathising nurse said to be responsible for it. Algeria must concede its place, his judeity must loosen its hold. The distance between the terrace and the city centre must deploy itself elsewhere. Thus pronounced, these words suggest that *the instant of being* proceeds from a movement of denial. On the contrary, framing it, imposing a fixity which was undoubtedly never its own, liberates the text from linguistic communitarianism, without reducing its *political* reach. If to love is to doubt, then to write is to doubt in everything.

...

"You sit at the foot of a mountain struck by the sea. Straight as a heron, white as chalk. I sit across from you, where I construct a reef of your pain in the sand, castles of larvae, a monument of bone. You touch nothing, you watch. // I gather pebbles that I offer to you like so many adornments. I trace the alphabet of birds on water. I pin your voice to the tinted sky. I wrap your feet in algae, I empty the place of its sorrow, I stroke the fish, I feed the turtles and calm the gulls. // I'm lying. I'm lying. I'm nowhere near."

...

Consolation is as much the *accomplice* of anticipation. Anticipation being the companion of deception. The resulting knot is mercilessly taut. All three—consolation, anticipation and deception—grapple with *expectancy*. Expectancy which is expectorant. The door opens. The hand is huge that grabs hold of everything. Everything is both the body and the name. History and its dissolution. Its secrets prescribed like a blood transfusion. From mother to daughters. From matrimony to fratricide. The small body on the doorstep. The less small body and the mouths nailed to the bed. Mathematically, you get: 18 months + 14 years. It is impossible to decipher. "I already knew that the intimacy of things is death. " (Bataille)

...

Jean Améry. Walter Benjamin. Rachel Bespaloff. Pierre-Alain Buhler. Paul Celan. Danielle Collobert. Geneviève Desrosiers. Josie Fanon. Hervé Guibert. Jennifer Haberman. Sarah Kane. Sarah Kofman. Primo Levi. Curt Lush. Alejandra Pizarnik. Ann Quin.   Stefan Zweig.

...

"Berlin, I imagined as much, but I too like not knowing. For the city to be nowhere and elsewhere at the same time." So B. means Berlin when he writes "this city." In July as at every other moment of the year, "this city" only materialises in the splayed space between two letters. This space is as vast and unfathomable as the sea beds and as narrow as a rivulet. "This city" is, of course, neither Berlin nor Lisbon, and locatable on no map, but takes form between two bodies writing one another across the inimitable distance of a friendship. These openings—these breaches—are particular to writing; intimacy opened onto a world caught off guard.

...

Transfigurations. In 2004, to have the experience of my trans-figuration such as I envision it at the time, I understand that I must learn to take my clothes off. So I get undressed, despite the advice of a psychologist I consult only two or three times, who encourages me to clothe myself further so that the illusion of my masculinity will be perfect. (A *perfect* illusion). Three years later, I encounter the necessity of getting dressed again to bring myself closer to the *disillusionment* of my body with its numerous fluctuations. It isn't because people don't look askance at me in the men's room that I am comfortable in my skin. The proof: in a small Midwestern city, I take a hike that leads in a direction other than the one indicated on the map, in other words, instead of a forest trail, a shooting range. It is worth pondering. I do not draw hasty conclusions by noting the degree to which *indeterminate* gender is endangered, or, in French, *en voie de disparition*—on the verge of disappearance. (Instead of *disparition*—I first typed *distinction*, which is much preferable). Distinction being that which is imputed by a gaze travestied by normality.

...

With some concern, I note a curious tendency, developed over the last three years in neighbourhood bookstores. My personal library being overburdened, despite regular purges, I find myself successively procuring books *I already own*. Yesterday, it was Walter Benjamin's *Illuminations*, in a 1969 edition, which, aside from the cover, resembles on all counts the edition, still from 1969, with an updated cover (a subsequent printing), that I bought a dozen or so years ago in Guelph. It doesn't stop there. After having sold a surplus of books, at the same bookshop—and because I was broke, not because the books were particularly troublesome—I nonetheless managed to bring home a copy of Walter Kaufman's translation of Nietzsche's *Beyond Good and Evil*, a copy identical to the one I had bought a month earlier at the same bookstore (and which remained unread). There are the two copies of *La force des choses* neither of which I have read cover to cover; twice *L'immoraliste*, twice *Le mythe de Sisyphe*, twice *Un tombeau pour Anatole*, three times (!) *Passages* (Ann Quin), two copies of *The Hour of the Star* plus a Brazilian edition that was as a gift (which is not at all the same thing), and very nearly two copies of *Écrire* by Duras which I narrowly escaped adding to my already laden bookshelves. There is of course the particular attractiveness of the *Livre de Poche* or old editions of the Gallimard "Idées" imprint (illegible, because the pages practically crumble as they turn, and the spines crack at the slightest articulation). The thing is I am not a collector, and this is the cause of my concern. I tell myself that these purchases are the product of an erroneous memory—because I have no idea they are doubles at the fateful moment of the purchase—but this realisation only masks an even more serious problem in my view, which is the silent demonstration of a crisis in the temporality of the body (mine, as it happens). It is that I wish to encounter these books *again*; some of them were first encounters, the experience of which I have not yet exhausted. This way of inviting amnesia into my library is disturbing, because when time catches up with me I am stupidly trying to overstep it, and the contortions necessary to accomplish this plant me firmly in the same affective abyss. The *nowhere*, the *there is not*, brimming with arrestation.

...

I would add to this a brief postscript. The collection of different editions of *Les nourritures terrestres* is not undertaken in error, but by design: I don't purchase every edition I find because I find some of them particularly ugly, but the intention that feeds this gesture is accentuated, not out of a desire for repetition, but for opening onto the multiple possibilities expressed by this text, arbiter of sensuality, *la volupté*—for which there is no just equivalent in English.

...

Because you love me you say: Nathanaël. You manage to put your whole mouth into mine. You offer me a book as though I had written it. You inhabit your city as though it were the entire world. I am your favourite faggot and you love me like a child: ragingly. There comes a time when you lose patience with the incoherence (your word) of our bodies, and so, to punish me you say: Nathalie.

...

Rimbaud: "Il nous a connus tous et nous a tous aimés."

A visual lapse has me substitute *abîmés* (damaged) for *aimés* (loved). Thus does the resolute chasm that preexists love, blood ties and affections (affectations) gape.

...

July 20, 2007: Cher B., // As usual, it is you that I turn to when words must slide out of my body, and find another (warm) body as a refuge. // I have isolated for you several passages from my manuscript, which, one way or another, enlivens the wound of Nathanaël. // I think you will understand, as usual. // I am confiding them to you alone, // As usual—// N.—// (*Prince déchu*).

...

Who among us has not been humiliated by one's own voice? The body attached to it pales, the fingers limply clutching the elusive, purloined moment. Myself, when I think of the cities I have walked through, I retain most especially a sharp disappointment at having encountered myself there. For one, the multiplication of voyages, travels, opens the world onto an infinitely pluralised possibility. But, and perhaps this is a constitutional flaw, for another (myself, as it happens), those same openings shut down one after the other as though behind me all the doors of the world were closing at the moment at which, naively, I would open them.

...

Jean Améry: "I have already spoken, alludingly, of capitulation, or, in other words, of the ineffectual fizzling out of esthetic associations and recollections. In more cases they brought no consolation, at times they appeared as pain or derision; most frequently they trickled away in a feeling of complete indifference."

Is there *collaboration* between capitulation and consolation? The connecting thread of aestheticism, capitulation might be the underside of consolation; one of its facets, aspects, modes, in other words always present and subdued. One way of unburdening oneself of the consequences of one's mediocre *occupations*. Out of this, this consoling *collusion*,

I retain especially the irremissible violence of abatement. The dissimulated layer of touch. The proximate brutality of declared loves. This isn't to say that love is capitulative, but that consolation is quite possibly the first lure of the fortuitous hours.

...

October 3, 2007. "I don't want to undertake this voyage alone, and since I have been considering it, I don't know why I never thought of you to accompany me. Given all sorts of things, including at least in part, your own difficult relationship to French, a proscribed state, a series of unendurable events, the inevitable deaths proving despite ourselves to be survivable and untimely, and the exhausted familial trope, vomited onto the poorly maintained facades of the past."

...

I say no, that death is mine.

...

Virginia Woolf: "Going up to bed we settled our quarrel on the stairs, and standing by the window looking at a sky clear like the inside of a blue stone, 'Heaven be praised,' I said, 'we need not whip this prose into poetry. The little language is enough.' For the space of the prospect and its clarity seemed to offer no impediment whatsoever, but to allow our lives to spread out and out beyond all bristling of roofs and chimneys to the flawless verge."

Books read us, fair enough. Languages borrow (from) us. What remains of the ruse of a used, of a disabused *I*? I go to you as I go to bed, to the sea, not to drown, but to interrupt, once again, the trope of my looking. So as not to stop. At a given subject or thing. A street corner. A delay. We tucked ourselves in to the floating sheets. The late-coming scars settle into what we call sleep. The thing that anticipates and awaits. We are astonished by the recognisable absence. A song whispered to an ear. May I call it a temperament? *Me duele*, says Spanish. *J'ai mal*, says French. And English: *I am in pain*. Expression of pain on the one hand ontological, habitational, on the other, possessive. Appearance, appertaining. Whatever we do, it lays claim to something. Pain constitutes itself in Romance languages; it acts on the body. Whereas in English it embeds in the self, undislodgeably.

...

Was Marguerite Duras's *douleur* constitutive?

...

Collobert: "a book/a form for all of it—momentary." *Une forme à tout ça.* Collobert knows she is dying, knows herself, to be, say, outdone. Collobert knows herself. Decides of that knowing. Determines *tout ça*—*all of it*. An overturned demonstrative? In the end, *ça* is as visible as it is knowable. The sign is also, might be, an alarm signal. A manifestation against reason, against know-how, the fait accompli. Is it necessary to undertake to deconstruct it? The deconstruction of *ça*? Objectively. I object that it is done. The goods have been delivered; they have found their form. Borrowed from the language of impasse. Because positioning oneself between fact and form supports an obliterating perspective. Of literature. And everything else—*all of it*. The flaw is of the order of tact. Of decision. In the morning in my bed, I awake tucked in strips of skin.

...

Vocabulary of traboules and casbahs. Secret passages, dissimulations. In 1982, I undertake by chance the apprenticeship of the interior courtyards. The city, comprised thus far of monuments (of grandeur), perched on mounts and pedestals, concedes its interiors. Of them, I retain the clay, a fountain, a cat stretched out on a window-ledge; but moreover the silence of these fragile places, inexorably tied to the war (but which one?) and evasion. The need to flee. I also learn that fleeing does not always mean leaving the borders, transgressing them, but stuffing one's body into the hidden recesses of the centre of the ancient city. Squatting in a volatile place, and waiting. The secret passage teaches me clandestinity. Mounts, flight. One and other seem interminable to me. Impassible.

...

I was born of an abduction. Unworthy and indignant. It goes without saying that the spiral staircase leading to the first floor was already catching fire when one of us was leaning over the balcony. Dubravka Ugrešić affirms that the return of the exiled to her country of origin amounts to a death; but that dwelling—implantation—is of the order of stagnation. All hope is determined by the movement of departure, the crossing of thresholds. No one lands on the sidewalk in front of the building. People enter, leave, go up, down. Here is the foul chronology of events: a note retrieved at reception, a fall on the stairs, an averted miscarriage, three successive departures, eighteen months of separation, an abandoned lover, a rape, several, three cities, two flights, a fire, two new beginnings, a daughter, excessive grieving, a split. Enough to make a magisterial denunciation. At present, the book is an accomplice to the same lie it is attempting not to conceal. Only now, the body implanted there has lost its voice.

...

I am dropped off in front of my apartment. I don't know where I am. I don't recognise the road taken nor the bar at the corner, I note that the bar opposite is strangely familiar, but the image stays caught in the strata of my thinking, where the exterior has evaporated, ceding its place to embarrassment: I know I'm disoriented. I recognise the disorientation and that is all. The words that anticipate me obliterate what they can of the present in favour of an avowal that surfaces without warning, carelessly. I have only to close the car door, cross the road, take the roads of four countries at least to reach the door corresponding to the key in my pocket, which will ostensibly open it. The way is blocked. The avowal made a clean sweep. Yes, I say and I repeat, yes, as though to reassure myself. Yes, to the city which catches in these slippages, despite the distance that was to have been tranquilising. I nod yes with my head. Yes. I disavow myself.

...

Desire that I desire. Not, this time, a desire for memory or obliteration, but reconstitution. I find myself at the edge of two rivers (the Mississippi; the Hudson); in a second-hand bookshop (on the way to Craryville), my back against a wall on a day of mourning (Potomac Street), on an electric wire, the bird you sing to me on a dirty sheet. This line uttered, unheard, unattended to: "Demented is the sea for not being able to die of a single wave." (Jabès)

...

The book of a kind of consolation could be written in the desert. A misunderstood desert in which books are deployed in the infinitude of regret and desolation. Hatred of dreamed landscapes, encountered, satiated bodies, the mouth made rigid by waiting. Unique condition of unconditionality: hunger.

...

But: "The desert has no book. The desert in which we are repressed by our powerlessness."

...

Malevich affirms that the "desert" is the place where only emotion is present.

...

Urban planning, surgical intervention. Haussmann's "grands travaux," Mussolini's *sventramenti*, Le Corbusier's Plan Voisin. Haussman takes pride in having destroyed 19,722 houses in Paris, 4,300 of which are in the old part of the city. Urban disembowelment needn't look far for its affective counterpart. Nomination, wishing itself monumental, razes the rest of me, the last of its effects, its unknown person. November 21, 2007, in a letter addressed to Michael O'Leary : "[...] this surgical procedure of disembowelment as applied to cities seems to me entirely related to this question of art; the figure is delineative; delineation is systematic, fixed; what the sventramenti did was to collapse everything into one devastated pit. I think that we have not emerged from it yet."

...

By the force of its fortresses, thought organizes itself despite obfuscating obstructions, surges and surprises—or perhaps because of them. The trauma of language is the very wager of our correspondences—of our "corps répondants." Bodies of uncertainty comprised of belches and vile gesticulations, shreds of nausea, weaknesses, each leaning into one and the same verbiage. Consolation might be a lure put in place to soften the unexpected, but nonetheless anticipated, devastation. Thus would consolation be akin to memory, the enunciation of memory (the body), in that it grants the *impression* of softening the sharp end of our sufferings. In other words, it permeates with lies. This does nothing to slow the vomitting; on the contrary, it probably provokes it.

...

The rage of this instant is the rage of every instant.

...

Finally they come for me. What first appears as an act of generosity—an unexpected gathering of people around a same affective edifice, say; friendship—turns quickly to condemnation. The ladders leading nowhere turn into a perilous rail, vertical falls and inclines that are just as steep, jouncing and summersaults, the train follows its infernal course, up and down and sideways, cutting through crowds, taking the same escape routes, fleeing, as do I, the many condemnations, death and threat. The site resembles a boarding school—dilapidated wood constructions, half-way between a dumping ground and a schoolyard; the allegiances are not clear. A hand is extended only to be severed. The chaos is the chaos of revolutions, genocides and parades. I recognise in the crowd, at the moment at which my throat is cut, the affable face of a friend. He is the one who helps me onto the train (or is it a coach) and whom I must trust when I am overtaken by vertigo and realise that this thing is unsupported outside of the assurance given me by the friend whom I must believe to get out of this accumulating, deepening, and complicating mess. Dream? Nightmare? In the end I call it: sleep. Because the nights make no distinction anymore, and the contusioned body traverses with difficulty, and without differentiation, the terrible days and the nights which are more terrible still. Waking and sleep would thus be two aspects of the same calumny, that of consciousness.

...

If I were to make a film, it would only ever begin. A stutter intercut with stutters. A voice suspended between breath and inflexion. Always at the edge of the film. Always in anticipation of the image. Because the image would be an impossibility. And the voice would embody that impossibility. Suspended precisely where the image could not materialise, could only subdue itself. There would be the voice—unexpected and interrupted—and the awaited image, so clearly superfluous. Does the refusal of the image amount to the refusal of the imaginary? To undo the imaginary from the unimaginable? Is such a thing possible? As from a lover or an aberration? To speak of love you cite time and speak your own name out loud. You cite time as a possession, a situation. What I receive of your transmission are swellings of sound, oral abscesses, drained and reconstituted in my own skin. This reiteration is neither echo nor capitulation, but the very error of the voice. The error of wanting to seize the voice on a soundtrack or in a mouth kissed several times.

...

December 7, 2007. "Melancholy days. We turn as in a cage. He thinks of the future he might have. I think of the present that is killing us. I'm not hungry and must force myself to eat. And you? Have you been able to rest? Tomorrow night I must present myself to the bourgeois to collect funds for my publisher. What role must I play? That of the seducer? The misanthrope? The social outcast? I don't want to. I have no appetite for this either."

...

Denise Riley: "Where amnesia would help us, we can't forget."

Forgetting in the face of obligation. Erosion fashions the lost, lasting passages. Where the instant is barely escapable. Whether the circle closes (Saint-Exupéry), opens (Saint-Exupéry again) or extends (Blanchot), it is the same stumbling cord, it is the same sprained tendon. The result is the same strangulation. Must this be called a tendency? Or contention? All I know is that there is a mispronunciation.

...

To make of the book of error the book of every possibility. Out of error, which would be both errant and erring, if not erratic nervosity, an entire other logic is deployed... unjust (pensée injuste, in other words logical, writes Camus). This *Notebook of Discord* has as its principle a failure, the failure of a book that cannot be accomplished, drawing into its wake the book of error as well as three unpublished manuscripts, one of which is unwriteable, the second of which is suffocating, and the third, admirably abandoned. In this sense, all possibilities amount to none. There, over there is the door which remains, for the time being, closed. I confront this observation which leads nowhere, if not into the most misleading meanderments. To take or to leave.

...

"Ella es un interior." (Alejandra Pizarnik)

...

Why books of immolation? I used to refer to the books of the present, those that comprise an improbable triptych, as books of immolation. What provoked such a declaration? The book of consolation was the first to receive the burden of that declaration. The horror of it must have resided, not in the accomplishment of the task (the production of a manuscript, then of a book), but in the resistance to it. Consolation, the unexpected, decomposition. Each corresponds with the two others, but neither divulges the existence of an interlocutor. Thus does the book of consolation become the referent of another book of consolation, the one that is written in the place of the one that cannot be written. The text of decomposition takes pieces from the two others, and the third, the manuscript which awaits the unexpected, has as its only expectation the illusion of its impermeability, which is to say that it is written without concern for the texts by which it is at all times being pilfered. The defeat is total. I am ceaselessly betraying one text in favour of another. None, of course, benefits from this betrayal, for all are destined to the same silence. It is in this sense that they are books of immolation. Where what is said is ceaselessly repeated; and what is repeated isn't said.

...

I have a friend who spends his evenings standing before his bookcases. He is waiting for them to collapse on him, burying him beneath refractory masses of texts. With just his hand, jutting through the pile, executing a futile gesture of supplication.

(Note: thus does the friend in question confide in me the

shadow cast upon him by the enlightenment by which we are said to live.)

...

One of the threads of Jasper Johns's work consists in an edge—the inferior edge—left untouched. Between the bottom of the frame of a painting and the painting itself, another, fairly thin edge, of unpainted canvas, asserts itself, an unequal distance, in appearances aleatory, between the fringe of the painting and the edge drawn by the frame. Infinite finishings. The eye slips, stumbles, catches itself in the space of this lure. In which the body is able, at its leisure, to dress or undress without infringing on its lines, without the anxiety of catching itself (being caught) in those gaping, solicitous interlacings.

...

A family matter: the genitor steals the child and the mother falls on the stairs. Because of this or not, he will repeat for sixteen years that the mother is dead. Another story: the daughter is born without a father, without bearings, and falls, at the age of two years, on the stairs. Because of this or not, the mother will make no mention of either the genitor or the brother. There is no relationship between these two falls, other than the mother's cry, torn violently from the dream.

...

Eva Hesse, sculptor of abstract forms that reveal themselves to be friable and subject to unexpected decomposition in the dwellings of their collectors (dwellings in appearances impermeable, but the simple atmospheric interaction with the works leads to their untimely disintegration; exhausted inexhaustible breath of material and subtle correspondences, fortuitous and crumbling), frames herself in an accessory dilemma. According to Lucy Lippard, Hesse relies formally and sensorially on the grid as both a prison and a safeguard. A paradoxical reach, then, whose restrained, girded force, walls itself in tensional elasticity, threatening the impermeability of the limits whose transgression (desired or not) is made underhandedly manifest by states of compositional erosion: that, of the body, which remains in appearances intact, comes undone upon contact with unsuspected influences, anticipated by the material itself.

...

To spare one's former self from shame, visibility. To spare oneself from who one is (abhors). I, too, know that "I am faced with a metaphysic of consolation" (Camus), but which one? Not the metaphysics procured by the nostalgia of revolutions ˙nor repulsed by them. I undertake the destruction of several papers, darkened, since 1988, by too many years. To thus collide, not with emptiness, but with the over-fullness of a life, an exhausted anguish, is to deny the transitional imperative of movement; the one that breaks distances and crumples the disavowals gathered despite oneself by one's attentive adversaries.

...

You collect countries like signs of approval. In the guise of offering, you place on my tongue: Barcelona, Turin, Los Angeles, Sarajevo. Still. In a forest in the north-east of the dubiously united states of your country, you begin to spit tears. For you, it is a way of marking your territory. Then, you begin to dance. They are one and the same. In both scenarios, I am there, but only insofar as I witness your solipsistic shudders. The hand you extend is the one that recuperates you. With or without me, you have the same fear, that you try to quell by throwing yourself around my neck.

...

Simply the year ends without any indication that it will improve or be otherwise. Benazir Bhutto has died, assassinated, and on Michigan Avenue the rush of consumers registers no disturbance. I only know that henceforth I will no longer wait in front of number 400 for the remainder of my day. Impossible to retrace the trajectory of that pedestrian adventure that for three years now has included the interminable corridors of the Merchandise Mart, the systematic surveying of the vast stretch of Millennium Park, tandem coffee shops, and the river's edge, overseen by the steel Trump monstrosity, without forgetting of course the raised passages of River North which sometimes end abruptly, at an impasse, at the edge of an urban precipice. Each step unwittingly recorded, culminating with the interruption of a sentence held in abeyance until a mythic and improbable next time.

...

"What do you do when the timer stops? I" (Pierre-Alain Buhler)

...

The injuriousness of incomplete works. That one may hold in one's hands a whole life of writing, organised chronologically, as though the logic of the book, tomes arranged systematically, with and against the ruptures, excesses, interruptions, the momentum of a life laid down now between the covers of one or several books numbered sequentially and imagining themselves to be definitive, could culminate in the regularisation of that which was characterised precisely, and at given times, by the unexpected, by concerns, hesitations, now calmed by a sober, restrained, tasteful binding. Must one see in the human effort to flatten a necessarily rough surface the "obstinate testimony of a life without consolation" (Camus)? But a testimony *imputed* by those who can say of themselves that they are still *there*. Yet this gesture, meant to be a mark of recognition, culminates instead in the enclosure of something that attempted in vain, for the duration of its life, the apprenticeship of breathing.

...

January 18, 2008. "By whose right does one forage in the intimacies of the dead? Carve out a warm place among their sufferings? My eyes are full of fog. Everywhere I see clouds that cover a disappearing world."

...

January 19, 2008: "...I know in anticipation that the violence of pain is reiterated by the mouth that pronounces these consolations."

...

"A holler in the place of a howl."

...

You say: "N., aime." To speak one's name is to be catastrophied, to offer oneself as an insult, an injury, a nominal cataclysm. To speak one's name is to concede the error of one's itinerary, the affected accident of the discourse that cannibalises by interpolating, to admit to the situation of a clogged flood, a plugged opening. The violence out of which is fashioned the name that coagulates one in the mouth of another, in a proper and intensified mouth, is the same violence of interrupted movement, of arrival without pursuance, it is the lure of both destination and the destined. To speak one's name is to await. But here's the thing. One arrives and finds that no one is waiting.

...

It was only with the arrival of R. that I was able to integrate an actual meaning to hospitality, to grant it a historical dimension, liminal, if not: linguistic. R. comes over and greets me *at home*, where I already am, all catastrophies combined. It is only then that the geographical (re) formulations to which I have devoted myself for many years become embodied, become newly tangible and that the advent of desire reveals itself to be still before me. One must travel very far to be received like this in one's own home; for the conventions to comply with chaos and reveal themselves to be disused and disposed, which is to say drained of meaning. Only then does the doorstep operate the slippages necessary for the unfurling of the foretaste of one's disappearance. In other words the disappearance to which each has a right is the unique guarantee of one's presence in a given place. It is in this sense that R. says to me, with great generosity: *you*.

...

February 22, 2008. "The time before, when we ate together at the Japanese restaurant, I swear to you that I was transported, in a moment of lucidity (or exhaustion!) into a distant future in which we were meeting like this but in a place unknown to me, for we were much older. Our laughter resonated similarly. What might it be, if not the irrecusable seal of friendship?"

...

Suffer and salve. A pressure exerted on a thing exacerbates its density. If the effect of porosity manifests now as fluctuation, now as reinforcement, against what must one lean in order to prevent the explosion? The fact is that the compressive forces don't tend any more toward eruption than they do toward sinking. In other words, the secret secretes. We live in conditioned anticipation of its seepage.

...

Nina Bouraoui: "We raise a wall, a prison within a prison. // We overturn a city."

Our societies function as afterthoughts, and we, citizens, are their posthumous evocation. This is not to say that we are still-born, nor that death conditions us (even if this is undoubtedly true), but that everything has simply anticipated us. To open what is closed would be a way to gather together the morsels that comprise us. Those bits of flesh attest to our disappearance. The self—saying I—in such circumstances, would be the avowal of one's posthumous condition, not of one's disappearance, but of obstinacy. This is the age of degeneration.

...

Place your bets.

...

Because you can think you're inimitable. Because you can very well claim no anteriority. Because the obliteration of the concept, "past," ends up eroding the embodied present. Because the sublimated borders are plied by the exigencies of a sublimated desire. Because, in the morning in front of the mirror, it is a face other than your own. And the tenacious conviction that the hatred reserved for others is the very hatred that devours you. That other who for thirty years misses and misspeaks.

...

A friend tries to situate limbo. He calls upon me as a witness, situating me there to begin with, in that undecided, undecidable place, and confirms, while asking me the question of place, that, according to him, I live between two hells. I think immediately of the crowded ferry that runs continuously between Oran and Marseille. 1961. 1993. Two hatreds, that manage repeatedly, and despite my waywardness, to reformulate me priorly.

...

When Camus affirms that he despises only executioners, he is taking on every geography and none. The incessant crossing to which the expulsed of Algeria are exposed.

But also the one which consists in a refusal to be dislodged. For each and other, the risk of attending the uninterrupted collapse of the present.

...

Must one bury oneself, if only summarily, with one's dead? Berkane (*La disparition de la langue française*) suspects as much. "After all," he insists, "if I had been an urbanist, an architect or a sociologist of urban space, it would have been necessary to live on the very sites of decline..." So be it. But what form would this dwelling take? For it to be able to accommodate its constitutive strata of violence. The rue du Regard must have an eyeful.

...

March 13, 2008. "Today I fell in love with you again. It's like that, some days you come violently to me, like a hard rain after a drought, and I wanted to write you many books more. *Paper City* deferred. Not necessarily Montréal. In another place where the whole day is assembled in the body to form a hard knot, a sharp pain, a wince, that dissipates in a rivulet of cold shadow at dusk, thrust from the mouth closed before the silenced enormity of the thing."

...

For the book of a certain consolation to realise itself, the very idea of consolation must be distanced from it. Left in the lurch: the book, and consolation. For the latter, having become uncertain, is transformed by its unspoken injunctions, and a source of powerful, incomprehensible and untiring disruptions. To raise the course of time is to drown of necessity; is to offer oneself to the sacrificial altar of anticipation. In order to say "in time," it is necessary to be amputated of the present. The neurosis of the country inculcated in the body is no longer a place of hospitality, but of recrimination. I move toward the idea the country has of me.

...

The gallows consists of three ropes, one French, another Canadian, the third Algerian. They form a single knot that tightens untiringly around the throat. The throat outstretched over heads bitten with curiosity.

...

1982. A door left ajar opens wide. For many years, one looks complacently through the keyhole, the judas, then opens slightly. A long sigh is released, it goes around the world. The sigh turns to a rattle. The door opens at last and the danger is produced. The wayward son enters and stupefies. This isn't a reunion, or an encounter, but an ambush.

...

I won't go.

...

"Now I understand why, at three o'clock in the morning, my breath was cut short. The idea of returning, maintained over all these pages, was savagely attacking the book, giving itself against the body, nourishing an unfamiliar rancour. Must I believe that, in these few years, I have been putting myself back on a wrong path, that of the desire for an imagined plenitude. I tried to call this consolation, but I know at present, having always known it seems, that one isn't revived at the source of a gaping, pustulent wound, even sutured. The steel hand gripping my shoulders that has been preventing me since this morning from breathing is the hand of a solicited convict. The force of mutilated things. Against my body the bodies of all my dead come to lie, and it isn't in the other land that I will retrieve them. It is in scattering that the present is made, and I am not prepared to mend it. // Must I postpone the voyage forever? I don't know. It is perhaps enough to be on the verge of undertaking it, without ever succumbing to it. For if there is return, there is also very likely defeat."

...

Three circumstances converge anonymously in August 2007. An interval of seven months amounts to this: a bridge over the Mississippi collapses, provoking thirteen deaths; blood lashes out in a body unconcerned with its mortality, provoking a hazardous diagnosis which is also the fruit of hazards, a rebellious cyst that propagates instead of shrinking; a circumstantial book proposes to follow the course of time backwards, which is to say to provoke, through the return to a banished place the release of an arrestation gripping the entire spontaneity of an illiterate body; by which I mean writing but concerned, this time, with its mortality, therefore having prohibited the slightest trace, including the one threatening it, with perennity. Three interrupted trajectories; three accidents denaturing the *passage* such as it wishes itself to be—*passing*. The first falls into the river; the second falls again and again into a hospital bed; the third in a language by which it is unrecognisable.

...

"Not malady. Maladaptive."

...

What would a present in accordance with friendship look like? The all-time functions like a prohibition against the shocks destined precisely to interrupt the will of friendship. Will rejects encapsulation ordered *against* the possibility of affective chaos, the role of the latter being to collapse that which imagines itself to be firm, unshakeable, massive. In this sense, all-time might resemble a short cut, without stops or exits, and visibly clogged. Me, I get off and I walk. I take my all-time and I tear it to pieces. I don't put anything back. I resist the doctrine of reparation, I take the road of breaches.

...

"His hand no longer responded to the brain's commands. It was his first death." (Roland Suzur, regarding Guy Hocquenghem)

...

In her first letter to Paul Celan (dated September, 1965), Ilana Shmueli cites this passage from Isaiah: "Console ye, console ye my people, saith your God. Speak ye comfortably to Jerusalem; and cry unto her, that her warfare is accomplished, that her iniquity is pardoned, that she hath received of Jehovah's hand double for all her sins."

That consolation (comfort) and combat should be in such close proximity, that the language of piety is also juridical language, is, if not egregious, then at very least desolating, and the lamentation seems a form as well of accusation. A consolation in the form of an accusation. An accusation in the form of a gift. The gift in the form of a nation. And five thousand years at least to detach from it, in imperfection.

...

At a friend's recommendation, I open V. I. Arnold's small yellow and blue book, translated from the Russian, and entitled *Catastrophe Theory*. Catastrophes are defined on page two: "Catastrophes are violent sudden changes representing discontinuous responses of systems to smooth changes in the external conditions." I immediately recognise that this little book which will in large part be incomprehensible will perhaps allow me another approach to the question of violence and its ontological component, if not its presence, that is—a question I've been asking myself for some time— whether ontology isn't itself founded upon an act of violence, the act of the situation of the self, of its rending, its distinction from, this thing called world. The act also of nomination. Whether, then, the constitutive act of ontology wasn't a violence. The violence that harbours the self.

...

March 25, 2008. "What kind of an ethic is borne of accusation? What kind of goodness is there in a doctrine of chosenness? When to be chosen is also to choose and when to choose is to have will and to have will is a form of freedom which is the freedom to do and to not do. And to be this thing which I am, which is monstrous, and cannot be otherwise."

...

March 27, 2008. "As for me, I shall continue to spit on the dead and to plant gardens."

...

Since 2003, I have noted several altogether aleatory equine occurrences in my readings, all the result of an unexpected encounter last December at a bend in a rainy road in Devon, on the moors into which, once I'd exited the car, I began to sink. (The sampling itself is aleatory, and not at all systematic; the encounter with the wild ponies of the moors was equally so.) There is Bachmann's "dying horse which had fallen off the cliff at Hermagor;" the coach horse of the Piazza Alberto de Turin around whose neck Nietzsche threw himself in tears as he was dying; another, Kateb Yacine's "smoking horse that roars in a horrid corridor;" finally, Guibert's, that calls and announces the void: "but I wanted to run, run like never before, at the equine abattoir, the beast whose neck has just been cut, continues to gallop across the void." Without, of course, forgetting Shklovsky's "knight's move" (literally: horse's march or walk, gait, in French), Koltès' "flight on horseback, very far in the city," and so on. Must we see in this animal and the sensibility it invokes, the misfortunate depository of human abjection?

...

April 7, 2008. "A wretched night. Forced myself out of bed this second. I dreamed dreamed dreamed. The man with painted eyes again. It seems inexorable now. (*A dream in a dream, a world in a world, a State in a State: such will be, once the signal is given, our general insurrection.* Yacine.) As though relief could only await me in that body. It's early, but the apartment is smothered in light, a light other than Edmund's, another adjustment. What I feel, if I am even capable of formulating it, is the compression in my body of all the pains, those from before, those to come. A boundless waywardness. I want to be elsewhere, or else alone, I don't know, at the edge of some water, in a place where it isn't my life that awaits me but the life of another, more vital."

...

Jean-Luc Nancy: "The setting in motion of place is identically that of the present instant."

...

To gauge the enormity of human stupidity, one need only spend a few hours at an airport. It quickly corrects the appetite to love.

...

"I think that I didn't speak to you of the young man with painted eyes; it isn't W.; it is, it may not at all be a person but pure fabrication. He nonetheless exists in the world and therefore in my dreams of holocausts intermingled with desire and disgust, and it would seem that our walk is permanently postponed. A dead dream? It isn't clear, and if I am to believe Nancy, not dead but *morendo*—"is not finishing; it is unfinishing."

...

In *La Ville Radieuse (éléments d'une doctrine d'urbanisme pour l'équipement de la civilisation machiniste)*, Le Corbusier presents "the horse without hoofs." It's another animal altogether. Jeanneret doesn't seem to see that the "mechanical caterpillar"'s passage "from the battlefield into the wheatfield" is annunciatory of the terminal phase of humanity. He is madly subjugated by (enamoured with?) the AUTHORITY to whom he dedicates his book, in which are presented architectural PLANS designated as DICTATORS. A whole hygienic program of moral restructuring chewed up and spat out by the timely Machine. Radiant City or Radioactive City?

...

"a real architect wants only to collapse the world." (Gordon/ Wilkinson)

...

My life is comprised of the reiterative translation of a single sentence (which isn't the same as a retranslation). Or a reiterative reading of the same book. The summer of the announcement of Ch.'s death (which never did, or has not yet, materialised), I announced that I would read only Sarraute for the rest of my days (*Entre la vie et la mort*). Happily, the days are counted, and the count collapses such that the result, reinforced innumerable times, indicates a swarm in the place of a single thing resembling all other things. Reiterative translation would be subject to constant transformations to make of it a translation indexed by multiple bodies including mine, never with exclusivity or exoneration.

...

There is neither filia nor filiation.

...

April 10, 2008. "I was in Chicago when he died or when I received the news of his death and the worlds burst apart again. I said to myself, that's it, we've lost our ability to speak to one another."

...

April 10, 2008. "Please forgive me. I'm very troubled by

this letter, and want to defend Derrida (it is not only the birthday we share, possibly a shared violence; it is possible that he gave me something I have since lost, that I haven't finished losing); some things can simply not be sung."

...

Impossible to grieve, to bring the body back to the present, to make an offering.

...

In September 2006, you make me the gift of the torn oceans, the sea. You dive and draw me to where the earth resurfaces, remakes the surface, a tear, to take or to leave. In your hands there are the oceans, the sea, and the tear that awaits me in your warm mouth combining sweetness and spit. Your geography, just like desire such as you practise it, is limited. It is impossible for me drown in it. Thus do I enter into it with obstinacy.

...

"...the West; I had preconceived a continent swallowed whole by geometry." (Malraux)

...

The time of de-responsibilisation is of all times. Whether it is the slaughter of "civilisation" (Hocquenghem), which, according to Jan Patocka (quoted by Derrida), doesn't exist, the refusal to forgive (Jankélévitch) where forgiveness has no business being granted (and where it is not asked for), there will always be "Paris which 'hurls its hatred at you,' Paris and its solitudes" (Ilana Shmueli to Paul Celan), Paris, (an arbitrary) figure of a cultural force, power and (therefore?) murderous, whose river is drenched with bodies, with falls and further falls provoked by an (in)visible hand. Must one see in this hand (that of Papon in 1961, multiplied through the forces of order, that of the multiple French and German gestapos, that of all the anonymous Clamences, distributed across every continent, resolutely, mutely, stuffed into his pockets, to cite just that one)—must one see in that hand the hand that writes, that gesticulates, that caresses and destroys?

...

The present subjected to a sort of wash.

...

For Etel Adnan, place is comestible. And is eaten with the eyes. "If we are what we see and the place we live in, then I am (...) these ravaged streets, this cadaveric smell that even fruits acquire when they start rotting, this disaster." If she seeks consolation near her dead, her friends' corpses, it is the proximity of the city, of cities, to her own body, that aggrieves her as much as the sea from which she is inseparable. "The books that I'm writing are houses that I build myself." That she builds (herself) with a concern for dilapidation.

...

A needle drives into the sister's wrist and splinters at the sight of the genitor. A smothered cry, wrapped in rage and flesh, or in raging flesh. Irretrievable, that same anger that grinds teeth and unabatingly repatriates the pivotal day on which the story of the abduction and continental drift might well have constituted themselves elsewhere, otherwise. ("(...) anastasis continues with the harshness of some cruelty to console." Derrida)

...

"The movement of the original is a displacement, an *errance*, sort of permanent exile if you will, except that it isn't an exile, because there is no homeland, nothing from which one has been exiled." (Paul de Man)

...

The error is not in erring—far from it—but in the appropriative gesture that leads a writer to make one thing out of two: the invention of the brother, he says, to explain the sister, ends up eclipsing the sister completely. Now I ask myself what eagerness compels the writer to instrumentalise the sister through the instrumentalisation of the son. To make the sister into the brother; to make that unequal relationship the pretext for a disappearance, that of the sister, whose existence now is dependent upon the brother who—twice—makes her disappear. First by offering himself as a means by which she might become *comprehensible* (legible). Next by eliminating the relationship of equivalency, even though it is binary—brother/sister—by referring solely to the bond ostensibly preceding it, the one binding it to a mother or a father, severing it from the sister who is not a daughter. Kinship precedes complicity; the juxtaposition of two bodies would serve only to place one at the disposal of the other for the purpose of being devoured. The writer's infraction is genial in that: the sister, excluded from all referential kinship, from all genealogical constraint, is free at present to rid herself of it, in the language of her choosing.

...

Is it possible to say of a building that it is sickly? I cross several fields, each more devastated than the last, and I climb the teetering ladder tendered to me. A curious ladder, several storeys high, attaching three city neighbourhoods while also detaching them from one another. It has one foot in an abandoned factory basement, the other set precariously on a wet stone, and we are a whole population to climb it. Having arrived in the garret of a very tall wooden construction, one need only lean out the opening to join the next field by way of a poorly constructed scaffolding. The impossible place of the dream is vertigo: between the worn wooden edge and the ephemeral structure which receives me in this impossibility. The terror of the dream is the terror of war camps and chemical products with which foods are saturated. All that is left for me to do is to consume my tribulations and study my sutures. I don't fall, I perish.

...

By some occular prolepse, my eye grabs a title in passing. It is F. Socher's *Manifeste néfaste* (*Nefarious Manifesto*). Looking more closely, I realise it is in fact a *Manifeste cinéaste* (film manfesto). This *in fact* is misleading; as though the correction of seeing were capable of some consolation. As though the fait accompli of the book could grant itself such certainty; as though the title held a truth that was—or might be—undivided. The eye, as it happens right now, far from being *misguided*, sets its sights on the book in all of its states.

...

May 1, 2008. "I'm going home now, I mean I'll cross the hall, and I'll be 'at home' in that grotesque suite with the two beds and the limits of my entire life."

...

You accuse me of so many qualifiers and counsel the middle ground. Indeed, I would like to answer you but the time difference disallows it, the middle is ungrounded and lacks justness as well (never mind justice). The qualifiers in question delineate and expulse, and that's likely what unsettles you in them. It's both the recollection—Jean-Luc Nancy's "One who comes to him*self* by hearing himself address words *as though* hearing himself cry (answering the other? Calling him?)"—and the waywardness of a banished body in the place of its banishment which, on a whim, decides at the last minute to retrieve the body from the total annihilation to which it was destined, while recalling it to its defeat and its duty. The duty to be silent, which could mean wanting without reprieve the rejected thing. Me, I want none of it, but it will leave me wanting nonetheless.

...

The news arrives from the other side of the door. Thus, in the summer of 2004, I don't move from the kitchen table for three days in a row. A country celebrates an anniversary no country is deserving of and I argue at length with a neighbour in a suburban garden. All it takes is one word for the thirty-three preceding years to revolt in a violent movement as far as possible from the body enfolding them. The third day, a faint scratching. An envelope slid beneath the front door. A border become suddenly traversable. "They tore out their hair, gouged their eyes, while opening a letter." (Catherine Mavrikakis)

...

Exodus. I find myself one day on the way to Toronto, where I'd exhorted myself never to set foot again, sprawled on the back seat of a car with my two dogs, my diaphragm seized, for several months now, by a painful constriction. Breathing, which had become an adversity, my body wanted only to fold itself in two, rip one end from the other, and be done with place altogether.

...

"A deep anguish all day yesterday, my whole body resisting return, and here I am (again), too soon, dismayed at having been torn from there. It is probably that very infidelity which had the cats complaining all through the night, as though to punish me for my excesses (...) the cemetery or your kitchen."

...

May 9, 2008. "... she told me things she'd said before and, for the first time perhaps, I understood what she was saying, and everything that had been incoherent became cohesive, and that coherence was unbearable because it's over now, the age of forgiveness and the need to ask for forgiveness. *Done with.* I suppose I never understood or never allowed myself to understand the tenor of the violence she experienced at his hands. A terrible succession. Now I have a mother and I'm not sure I really know what that might mean nor how I'll manage to understand the presence of a mother after the refusal of the possibility of a mother, not to mention the solicitation of an impossible mother."

...

Stop it. "But you have the power to console us of what we were." (Catherine Mavrikakis)

...

May 9. "There is lily-of-the-valley in the garden, a single stem, stolen from the foot of the neighbour's stairs last fall. // There are one out of three hyacinths, white. The squirrels ate two bulbs and left me one."

...

May 9. "When I imagine the letter I would write you in French, I tell myself that the only possible letter would be a letter from Marguerite Duras, that I would write you. That particular madness."

...

February in May. Says my name, Nathanaël, that I no longer recognise for not recognising the face that produces it. My name Nathanaël offered anonymously as though to relieve me of it. It wasn't a matter of dreaming of "the boy with his wrong name," or of the "name with its wronged boy" (Gordon/Wilkinson). What revivifies me is neither error nor issuance, but embarrassment. That astonishing embarrassment that collapses the body in an unapproachable place, where the lips graze a mute, incapable sound. "For eyes were necessary to see them but hands also to take them." (Yves Bonnefoy)

...

A possible architecture of desire: upright body leaned against a hot pipe (winter) in a cold room; tabula rasa to linger over (torment); overturned taxi on a major street (rupture); stairs, institutional corridors (immanence); floodway (fury).

...

Claude Cahun: "Write me letters the way you know how: alive, moving, the illusion of a presence—." Letters supplant "literature." It was about time. The organisation of the text in this form referred to as a book lied as to its origins and its descendance, its surge and its depletion. And yet it isn't a matter of discarding the two covers and the pages over which to linger. Because the thing referred to as a book isn't a tangible thing but rather of the order of an apparition. Irreducible to the number of pages or the thickness of the binding, the scale of the *press*, but volatile and scattered.

(Small divergence: *press*, one of the French equivalents of which is *appui* (support), but not in the sense of an exact equivalence, rather of an approximation. The book in this sense leans on me at the most fragile point, threatening to crush me under its inadmissible weight, which is to say that it isn't capable of admitting its weight, any more than I am able to measure it).

...

I must remember you as someone else. This isn't an injunction, but a supposition. That I remember you as someone else, not out of necessity, but for having left such an efficient blank in the place of our first encounter, which I don't remember at all. Thus does the "I must" occupy both a space of condition and supputation. Occupation and disappearance. I make no promises. Not error nor recognition. I say that Claude is an impossibility. I tear him from the mouths of others.

...

It was something else again. *The Notebook of Discord* could just as easily have been the notebook of another thing, of things otherwise. Other, of course, than the intentional book, the given book. Will of consolation, in the urgency, perhaps, of an inconsolable gesture, that knows itself to be inconsolable. (Epistemology of reprieve? Logic of appeasement?) Precisely, being-inconsolable is neither becoming nor destroyed and certainly not calculable. Unless I am mistaken, being-inconsolable is both the condition of and conditioned by *an other thing*.

...

The "may-be," is both the un-predicted and the un-prevented. The gross and seductive awkwardness of enunciation. The "may-be," is the after-effect of the landings of the great wars (is every war not great). It is thought after the fact, unreflective, always obstructed, in the face of a possibility exceeded by the events. Claude, the child on the rooftop, owes his potentiality to his death (which calls up *more*—or excess, because, unjustly, of its unfathomable *and* absolute quality). He owes his potentiality to his damaged death, his piecemeal death, masticated in so many familiar (familial) mouths biting into him after the fact, including mine, which robs and surveys him with a hazarded desire to remove him from the roof where I imagine him in mute conversation with the birds. As though this gesture could free me of the constraint of being loved (appropriated) in detestation and filiation. To remove the other, already dead, so as not to repeat the error of descendance—the error, precisely, of *expectancy*?

...

Claude occupies the place granted by death. There is a torn photograph of him. There are vaguely discernible doors. There is a grey rain. That returns what it can of the past. That blanches the sidewalks and ruins the outmoded archives. // I take it all into my bag. I say that the circumstance is illegible, wrecked. I say it and say it again. Claude faints in my limbs. I kiss Claude on the belly.

...

In Hebrew, the verb "to be" is not conjugated in the present; it is elided. Thus: *Ani talmidah* (I (am) student). The pronoun, become transitive, contains the "may-be" of transitory, intransigent subjectivity.

...

"No category ever will contain me." (Thierry Hentsch)

...

There is the vexation that prevents. Prevention is of the order of resistance. A resistance to a silenced thing. The silenced city finds that it is every city. It is no longer possible to distinguish between one place and another place. It is this very confusion which provokes the dismay of the present. The surge that turns the body over. The overturned body is and is not mine. Mine for having crossed so many borders. Not mine for having ended up where I am not.

...

It had to come to this. For arrival (I hear you say *And you, you have only just arrived*) to be the arrival of the present, in the present. For the spatial preoccupations to result in the anguish of temporality. In the *there* that has no concern with situating itself but with its own enunciation, making of place a word relegated to later. Later being the place one doesn't arrive at. One is determined by the other: which is to say that place must be spoken for the body to be able to situate itself there and, in order to speak itself, for the body to have an idea, not of what it is, but of where it is. If place results necessarily in no-where (only one of the possible acceptions of *I don't know*), that explains the prevention and vexation, even the arrestation of speech. (Speech, which must be distinguished from writing, what is written, even indistinctly. Writing is not, will never be, the graft of a spoken thing on a piece of paper but the distance, the disjuncture, the irreconcilability between the desire to speak and the impossibility of speaking, whence the need for writing, to enable the body, with and because of its binds, to be smothered otherwise, here as elsewhere).

...

The quotidian ruins everything.

...

May 19, 2008. "Barely a week and I'm already there. Breathless with admiration for the volcano. Is it even worth reminding myself that by gathering this distance into my legs, by returning my body to the site of language, it escaped me immediately?"

...

May 20, 2008. "You know, the fact that I can't make up my mind to settle here, I experience this as a failure."

...

In Montréal I find the same sky as in Chicago. Only there do I begin to understand that it is the same pain, the same cruelty, distributed over several ages, in several places, never the same, always the same.

...

Spring 2008. The eyes are torn by looking. An unbearable thing settles itself. Dust on the retina. Drownings.

...

C'est tout. L'oeil et l'esprit. Apprendre à vivre enfin. On the Concept of History. Il donc. A hora da estrela. Schneepart. Les damnés de la terre. Mille pas dans le jardin ne font pas le tour du monde. Dictée. Pour un tombeau d'Anatole. L'étrange défaite. L'amphithéâtre des morts. Hiermit trete ich aus der Kunst aus. Ouvrez.

...

When a pair of translators contend, with regard to a text of Joseph Beuys, that they are reproducing a discourse in its "quasi-integrity," without further explanation, I am already suspicious of the text (and its translators)—even more than usual. How am I to situate myself in relation to this "quasi" integrity? What has been suppressed? Added? Reformulated? "Corrected"? What exactly is a "quasi-integrity"? How is one to trust this thing which says it has been manipulated, beyond the expected (and unexpected) manipulations of a translation. Given especially that the biographic note opening the book indicates in addition that 'Beuys's language is now abstract, now concrete. It is personal, sometimes at the limit of comprehensibility. The translators, confronted with this dilemma, have chosen intelligibility.' What is this so-called intelligibility that is being imposed on me? If I am reading Beuys, it is likely precisely because I want to rub up against the *limit of comprehensibility*. I consider the role of the translator to be precisely to hold simultaneously in his or her hands the abstract, the concrete, the personal *and* the limit of comprehensibility. And not to excise the thing that hinders him or her in that work. I once decided against reading a book by Georg Simmel translated into English for this very reason. The translators, anticipating the stupidity of Anglophones, decided to simplify a text that was in their opinion too complicated. We can agree on one thing, the untranslatability of every text. But when the translators insist on censoring the reading of an author, to inflict us with this multiple violence, so as not to agree to break themselves at the place where languages are confronted with one another, I can but concede the anticipated stupidity of the translators.

...

To write is to give one's word. To give one's word (to the other). To make a gift (of oneself) to speech. Until speech gives in. Is given. To give in to speech would thus be both an act of generosity and a capitulation. To take it would be to take responsibility for it. To assume that which, of speech, extracts and imposes (its law).

...

Speech: on the verge of tears.

...

If I give my word (if I put my hand to the fire), I understand that I am inconveniencing others. The indignant young man who accuses me of making books that are undone (for him, lacking resolution), accuses me in sum of having given him my word. He does not want to have to assume his responsibility. He does not want for the text to do anything to him other than that which he believes it already to be. A foregone conclusion. In other possible words, consolation is necessarily nailed to accusation (like Abraham to his son, and to his mean little god, to his sin). One never leaves the other. Speech strangles writing. Writing is that thing that leaves the body despite—perhaps even because of—strangulation. Undoubtedly, yes, because of strangulation. *"If you speak you die, if you do not speak you die, so speak and die."* (Tahar Djaout.)

...

Accusation and adoration. Had he not existed I would have invented him anyway. I would have found a way to invent him so that he would have stopped threatening to exist.

...

"Art is wretched, cynical, stupid, helpless, confusing—a mirror-image of our own spiritual impoverishment..." (Gerhard Richter) I open the red recycled paper notebook, with its inconsequential title. This notebook, which was once a book, and serves in 2004 to retain what overflows from some of my reading. I turn the page and fall upon this, the last sentence that I could be bothered to copy down that day before plunging into Lippard's book on Eva Hesse : "Consolations are sold: all shades of superstition, puffed-up little ideologies, the stupidest lies." I am in Montréal now. I found the Richter in a painter's studio in Chicago in 2004 while convalescing in Toronto. The question of the book of consolation was only just beginning to (im)pose itself. In anticipation, I was seeking to undo myself from it; I was already accusing its absence.

...

In the public square, impossible to hide. I manage nonetheless to take cover in the bushes to remove what needs removing. Is it because of clothing and sleep, the heavy sheet that provokes impotence in the body in the middle of the day. I don't know. I just know that, when the time comes, I painstakingly extract the rag stuffed down my throat, thick with vomit, like a cat perhaps. I say this, but as far as I know, cats don't vomit rags. Plant leaves, yes, and fur, but not rags. In my case, it's a rag, a towel that exits my stomach through the mouth, a thing preventing me from breathing and that I can't expel. Having accomplished my task, I lift my head and it's the whole public square staring down at me with disgust.

...

May 24, 2008. "É. says he reads me in English especially, which surprised me, because I must write better in French.

That's how I see it. I'd give all my books published before 2003 to burn. Except for *Underground*. But it is also true that for a version of history, I'd tear my face off."

...

May 24. "That's where I want to be, in the plus-present."

...

May 24. "As far as existence is concerned, you are right to ask that question. I ask it myself. Today I wondered: do I exist? And I told myself that I ought to ask others the question as well. Maybe that's what I am doing all the time. I am asking others whether I exist."

...

May 25. "I was simply exhausted. Épuisée. And this morning again, very tired. The exhaustion that draws lines under the skin along the left side of the face, drawing the eye toward the chin. Like an extended tear, silent. Invisible. Je t'assure. Believe me."

...

I am convinced that I am on the verge of bumping into

him. On the street, exiting the métro, in front of my place. Here, wherever, whenever. I think it in my dreams, since they announce this encounter incessantly, this encounter that I don't want and from another point of view I don't care about at all. The first time I did want it. All of us, we all anticipated it for fourteen years at least. Since before my birth and my sister's. Which explains in part that it was also catastrophic. It was very simply the advent. The advent of the son and the brother. The advent of a repressed violence that was exploding, that needed to explode once and for all. Now I know that I am probably the one who is inventing it. That without this, I would have invented him anyway. On the doorstep, I invent the door, and the place such as it declares itself.

...

"On the contrary, we have perhaps always been strangers one to the other and this is what makes these encounters possible, again and again."

...

Freedom does not exist outside of the constraints imposed by the fragility of the body. It is precisely through this fragility that freedom passes.

...

May 26, 2008: "It would have been necessary for me to write you in French directly. To trust this gesture, this desire to meet you in that language, as we would meet at the foot of a hill, at the entrance of a subway station, or walking somewhere, simply. It is possible that I am grieving this all the time, grieving not being able to meet you there, to meet several people for whom French will always be an inaccessible space, and it is that space, an encounter in that space, that I am grieving. For I know that even in translation, interpretation, I am not able to say the thing that is being said, to transmit it properly, and that I too incohere at the very place where the conversion takes place, at the moment at which I undo the thing from one language to do it up in another. It is not the language that is lost, but me. I lose myself at the place at which the traversal is undone—defeated."

...

"I mean to say that it's me, it's me that I'm grieving, and French."

...

A beat in the blood. A language that is unfamiliar to me.

...

Enough poetry and novels. Those resolutely surveyed territories. Those paralysed spaces suffused with smugness, which eradicate themselves as they are erected. Speak to me instead of what eludes genre, of what eludes situation, of what, of myself, I don't recognise, that morcellated language cast to the wind, that bruised body lacking a destination, which lands somewhere over there, far from the noise of demonstrations. Who has not yet understood that the risk, there, of the nation—of territorialisation—is also that of the literary, the littoral, plottings.

...

It lasted roughly six months. You presented yourself to me, inescapably. Entirely embodied. Body in excess. All-body. It was one of the first things I noticed, that held my attention. I was detained by your corporeality. You required a presence of me and I understood that that presence depended upon you. From that moment on, I began every day to take pictures of myself, in order to convince myself that I existed outside of your gaze. Outside of the gaze I directed at you. Infinitely deported, displaced, projected, in the *I* of the other, in the *I* that I was usurping at the expense of an already destabilised capacity to say (to myself) the thing, there, me. That I existed once and for all. Those photographs don't resemble me at all, or else yes, but always with sufficient deformation such that the question of resemblance must be posed, with the gaze, there, detached, detaching.

...

Correction : grieving French, grieving that which French cannot—does not—want.

...

What I retain most of all from a Ionesco or a Beuys is very much their individualism. Their distrust of the collective. Of that form called crowd—whether constituted or not— which is unleashed without regard for the consequences. I admit to having difficulty distinguishing between the crowds of Pamplona running the bulls or pilgrims piously climbing a mountain, their knees in shreds, all are questioning some same thing that eludes them; or even some militia mobilised to lay down the law, a law. Always the law of an other.

...

The smell of coffee burns my eyes.

...

"It was probably in the time of writing *L'absence au lieu*, which happened during the six months following the talk given in February, and it rained in the morning such that my boots were soaked and I squelched noisily through the vast rooms of the Musée d'art contemporain, and on my way back the city was ice and wind, the temperature having dropped some twenty degrees centigrade, the wind at 70 kilometres an hour, something L'Ami bemoaned that very evening, saying it was difficult enough as it was, what with my tortured relationship to the city, and he apologised in its place."

...

The country wanted for me and thus did it resent me.

...

Evidence. When I find myself before a work by Anselm Kiefer, I'm summoned by an unbridled masculinity—and Germany. When he repeats Speer's grandiose efforts, for example, to elaborate an (implicit) critique of Speer, he is obviously situating himself in his wake. In the wake of a fallen body of work whose amplitude is catastrophically untimely, omnipresent. On the anticipated ruins of Speer, the empire of Anselm Kiefer?

...

I go to say: I miss you. Instead I say: I resent you. Rancor comes immediately to fill the absence.

...

"... do you know how much man is 'yourself? imbecilic? and naked?" (Bataille)

...

The organisation of space is such that in 1982, bodies and sexes can only be accomplished in discord. Impossible to do otherwise. Of the two possible sexes, only one is retained: the sex that will inhabit the space. Beginning with the bookshelves and ending with the bed. Beginning or ending, we always end up there.

...

June 2, 2008. "Three weeks already. Death must be just like that. One day a train station, you look at your watch and say to yourself, so soon? // Je t'embrasse. July, then—"

...

"Names change place in my mouth."

...

"The *I* is sometimes in the masculine. I hesitated. By turns I chose Sarraute's 'neuter' and my own exhaustion at having always to choose. An exhausted *I*. I tell myself that Romance languages would do well to do away with the feminine altogether, so that we can all gather around a same divergent speaking."

...

The dissolution announces the possibility of new forms.

...

Concede nothing to convention. "Poetry like bread?" asks Bachmann. "That bread should grind between the teeth and awaken hunger before appeasing it." We aren't at our first word, nor the last, but at the blandly resembling. And if we were to agree to resemble *nothing*?

...

Wayward letters: fall 2003, a letter sent from New York to Montréal, addressed erroneously to Montréal, NY, doesn't reach its destination; winter 2006, a stem of creosote sent from the desert is diverted by an aleatory wind; fall 2007, a book sent from Toronto to Chicago is lost somewhere between the red door and the green door; spring 2008, a postcard sent from Côte-des-Neiges to Brooklyn hesitates at the border; fall 2007, a book sent from Wicker Park to the Plateau makes a detour through Zurich—the seal attests to this—to arrive a month and a half later at its destination. This is the only envoy to reach a letterbox. In at least four postal stations of this continent, there is a blue letter, a wilted stem, an illegible book and a card from which "à grands cris" Camille Claudel demands her freedom. Letters taken at their word?

...

"It's perhaps because I never really learned how to speak. In one language or another. The book serving as a mediator between the body and the world. If one can even say of this 'between' that it exists."

...

I despise Mozart. Anathema! But I'm prepared to suffer the consequences of my avowal everywhere and for always. It is Mozart's mathematicity that is so unbearable. That irrevocably *calculated* music inspires boundless disgust in me and makes me grind my teeth. I turn it off to commune instead with Mola Sylla's voice that gently crushes Reijseger's compositional limits, one with the other at times, and it is precisely this indistinction which enflames my suffering and my joy.

...

At present, the countries are detaching from the maps. A thread twisted at the foot of villa Alhucemas, tendered to

Lyon, via Oran—three wars in tandem, the Rif, Vichy and the Algerian War—begins to unravel for good. A wall crumbles, the teeth crumble in the head of the one who would like to continue to speak, speak, cry, speak, and for myself, I retain just the entangled accents (Spanish, Arabic, French), dead for so long in time, a tetchy time that goes back some twenty years, that this amalgam of words and emotions, *Aï-ma, aï-ma*, the open hand pressed against the chest to prevent the body from bursting, that all the lands may be cleared at once, and seven adult children, aged sixty to eighty years, on the verge of being orphaned, grope toward one another.

...

Accusers of the last century.

...

I lied. I killed two manuscripts (many more than two, but pertaining to consolation, two, it seems). Stowed strangled asphyxiated. There was a murder, it's true, more than one. The book dead in the body of the animal also killed the animal as it died. What animal? We are so many.

Chicago, Montréal
June 24, 2007–June 8, 2008

...

P.S. The third elegy of Romanian poet Mariana Marin asks the question: "Do you wring the poem's neck / when you discover it inscribes itself even without you?" (I consider the neck of poetry to be very well wrung, or else insufficiently so). Her translator, Adam J. Sorkin, indicates that these elegies "do not mourn, let alone console, as much as condemn and castigate." Thus, between two smothered words (Marin's and her translator's, smothered by what if not the noise of history, "history from way back when"?), are the grotesque and indecent aspects of (poetic or other) consolation exposed. Like those furs that for several years now have come back into fashion, and that some don to exhibit the violence of having, the slaughter of being. Their eyes cast repeatedly over a shoulder, aware that they're vested in their fault. (June 11, 2008)

The provisional advantage of the word "brother" over every other word designating that which binds someone to someone is that it is drained of all sentimentality, of all affectivity; or, in any case, it can easily be rid of it. It can be hard, aggressive, fatal, almost said with regret. And then it suggests irreversibility and blood (not the blood of kings, families or races, the blood that is quietly enclosed in the body and which has no more meaning or colour than the stomach or the bone marrow, but the blood drying on the sidewalk.)

—*Bernard-Marie Koltès*

DELIBERATION
(Quasi una fantasia)

I came across the piece of paper from a year ago which was wrapped around *L'impossible* and I set about writing you a letter, which I had intended to do ever since that paper had grazed my fingers. Only today, looking more closely, I find there an inscription in your hand, which had escaped me until now. Twice then I receive this from you. And so it is impossible to inscribe anything at all and send it back to you. Instead I preserve it in an uninscribed folder. A blank folder so to speak, in which there is everything of you including the desire to respond.

But since I and I we will die, you don't doubt it, there is a structurally posthumous necessity of my relation—and yours—to the event of this text which never arrives at itself.

—*Jacques Derrida*

… But we can already hear the beams cracking. It is night before day and the fire is lit at dusk.

—*Ingeborg Bachmann*

They said that what they were looking for was to be themselves, and that I had succeeded in being me, and that to succeed in that is a suicide; it was a suicide of all the other possible selves.

—*Marguerite Duras*

The second reason lies in the fact that the knight is not free—it moves in an L-shaped manner because it is forbidden to take the straight road.

—*Viktor Shklovsky*

The roofs fly off. From the window I see them rise into the blue of the sky, those decapitated edifices, it's my life flying to pieces.

...

—*Horror vacui*. Horror of the beyond sustained in the world.

...

First I think that I am grieving you. Then I understand that it isn't that at all. Everywhere I go I revivify your presence on these roads so that the city doesn't lose sight of you. When I say that I am retracing your steps, it's in anticipation, and not in order to signal a fait accompli. Your death, for example.

...

I don't imagine myself *elsewhere*, because elsewhere, I realise quite stupidly, doesn't exist.

...

I must make a note of this somewhere. Say it. So I entrust

it to you, you. (Please forgive me).—Tonight he said to me: if […], I'll stop. Stop.—And me, through the window, I wonder, but what do I […]. Where exactly ? Where ?— (*L'Injure*: What are you left with? If not the smothering, inexecutable desire, to name.)—I'm suffocating. There is no air. Not inside, not outside.—Often […], it's too painful.—I had told myself […], , but not sideways.—Now I am before this notebook, and it's all that wants to come out. The dam will burst.—I'm devoting my full force to its restraint.—Its reprimand.

...

When I speak, I don't necessarily hear myself. I mean that what comes out isn't rigorously certain of its provenance, of the provisional origin that might be a body, isn't able to speak (itself) while speaking (of) itself, that this thing here comes out of a me, a so-called self. The schism between speech and the act of speaking is sometimes terrible, and so as to become unburdened of it, one designs mechanisms of estrangement to rid oneself of that which might bear one some resemblance, by excess, or misfortune. The excedent is sometimes also the *refusal* of recognition.

...

There is no longer: *elsewhere*. So goes the dictatorship of possibles. It won't have been necessary to represent it with a figure; a wall, for example, or a barrier. Simply, the effort sustained to project oneself toward another place is *inconsequential*. The place other than this one is just as much the place of death, and of decomposition. To say *I*, then, by which I mean to install oneself *elsewhere* in language (whichever one), or to exchange oneself against several, leads to the seal of one's possible disappearance, at every moment inconceivable and decided.

...

I sleep against you. The shore is murky, foul. You are soaked. As am I, soaked, on the jaundiced, delapidated shore. Gravel, waste, water. City, not-city, I don't know. I sleep againt you, you're dead, suicided. Hanged, I think, yes, I note: hanged, but you are soaked through as though you'd come from this water, laid out on this shore devastated by abandon. You don't sleep, neither do I. Stuck to your skin are dirty strands that also stick to me. Long wet strands of brown, soggy string, unkempt shores, everything grey, brown, hair, bits of rope. You cling to me without touching me. I say nothing, I shout, sob, choke. Nothing. There is nothing to say, there is only this act of love. You fuck me. Dead, you take me. In death, there is only this filthy, gentle, wracking love. A decomposing love. I come and I wake on a gutted pillow. For nothing, I say.

...

There are no futures anymore; a present without possibility. Strange the way the skies close in and distance is repealed.—

[…]—Thank you for your letter and the letters underneath. I've pinned them each into my skin.

...

Tuesday, the acupuncturist asked whether I was […]. I was going to say no, but I said yes instead, and I think I answered well. But even […] (if that's really what it is) hardly holds my attention. So I read and re-read Nietzsche to dispense myself of it.

...

[…] I think that this encounter unleashed a soft furore in me.—[…]—For this reason alone, I follow his gaze.—It's a good thing I'm saturated with shame, otherwise I might have come closer.—[…] don't counsel me reason. I've become rabidly prudish, and desire dismantles me.—His lover is […],—As for me, I was quiet,—acquitted

...

That's probably where I should plunge, situate myself, in this derailing text, open the floodgates, and inundate the residual areas.

...

—The only possible freedom is unthought. The eventuality of hope depends on it, the hope of figuring a death, of drawing its outline for oneself. Mavrikakis: "We are free to do as we wish with our characters. We are sad, immensely sad, but free. Do you understand, girl? Free, even in the violence and the horror that beat down on us. Free to give death the doddering sense that suits us."—Guilty lapsus; inside this sentence, I find: *libres de donner la mort*. (Free to give death).

...

Overtures—The scene builds at the rhythm of the conversation. Empty terrace. One table, two bodies. And the astonishing choreography of the conversation. One changes place to smoke, sitting, then, across from the other, body sideways, soberly calculated gestures. Offer of the force of his twenty years. Boulevard that borders the gated terrace. Passers-by, automobiles. One wears a black shirt, sleeves rolled up, the other an orange jacket. One, across from the other, consulted, scrutinised.—Gaze onto the boulevard. Foliage illuminated by headlights. Inhalations. Their late bodies. Philosophical consultations. Rigor, abandon. Simone Weil, Jean Genet. Concrete tile. Black tea, coffee. Implacable fence against a backdrop of purple sky. Feature-length. One hundred and forty-four minutes, give or take, aside.—Retake. Focus on the bodies in movement. One: rises and moves, changes place, takes time, rises and sits down again, across, sideways. The other: remains, expectant.—

...

And if I succeeded in being the *subject* of no discourse; if I succeeded in escaping the mechanisms of enclosure and control such that their outlines and mine would all dissolve. For *subject* is forcibly akin to subjection, the pronominal irons determining the positional eye. You confide to me your desire to be a centaur, detached from the linguistic restraint that traces its habitual furrow between the field and the stable. I don't answer. Unbridled centaur, subjectless, I follow.

...

Nominal equivocation. I sometimes sign N/N (*nomen nescio?*) By inadvertence, I fall (again) upon an iteration on this doubling, NN, which isn't actually foreign to me: *Nacht und Nebel*. What must be drawn from this circumstance, this accident which may not be one? I anticipate the sighs of exasperation, the refusal of this accident in particular, the objection of my predilection for catastrophe. And yet it isn't a matter of crudely gorging myself, of taking affective advantage of this historical abyss, but to recognise that even the most wilful expression of desire (contradiction), of the deployment of an interrupted repetition—cut by its own breath—exceeds its intention. That too might be called freedom. Compromised freedom. Is freedom not compromised *anyway*?

...

I must be going mad, no doubt, more than ever, not an extravagant madness like the madness of my twenties and which, I now recognise was not a madness at all but a fervent, vital relentlessness binding me paradoxically to existence, the senses, to the mortal insanity of the desire to touch everything, to renounce nothing. No, at present, this madness is a madness of detachment, in which the world, enclosed, excluded, has entered into my body in the form of an illness which does not belong to me, that I continue to ingest until I cannot distinguish myself from it. Like Guibert, perhaps, I have become the lover of a morbidity... for me, latent, outside of myself.—So much for your bastard friend. Buffeted, bound.—

...

I say nothing about you. I don't skip any steps. Only sometimes I situate myself where you already were not, that is where neither one of us was disposed to address the other. For lack of naming. The dream disrupted everything. *Already* was equivalent to *after*, one unfounded the other, and the arrival of the name interrupted by our stuttering implemented a temporal fashioning in the real that neither of us was capable of assuming. The body, however, took it into account, and when you leaned against me, the infinitesimal adjustment of coordinates constellated us otherwise. If only language had been able...and us with it. Exile is such that together we were only able to observe: love is posthumous. The question, thus posed, was forcibly gaping.

...

The life of a centaur must not be easy, but I imagine it full of possibles—what is it if not an unsutured question without the *possibility* of an answer?

...

(It's true that if I were to write you in French, I would say things differently, I might be (slightly) less timid, I would open a book and read you a passage, a passage suspended by the interruption that convokes both of us, abandoned there, at the door, at the moment of leaving. You see—)

...

At the age of one hundred a woman rises from her bed for the first time in several years. She begins by refusing to speak to her children. She sums them up: in one century, thirteen labours, she belabours the point. Conclusion: thirteen existences in varying stages of disintegration. So much for the *gift* driven into *duty*.

...

—I couldn't say, and distrust my reasonings, because everything, it seems to me, can be reasoned, and at what point must one let go, or rather what might letting go signify, especially when one is barely holding on and when the part of the world that takes hold, in relation to the idea one has of it, is only disjuncture and estrangement?

...

What could I grab hold of just now to prevent from drowning? Lie down on the ground for it not to open up? I wish I were concrete or frozen mud at the centre of a forest. Brimming with suspended frogs.

...

—This morning at four o'clock (because I am no longer able to sleep by this new schedule), we forgot the consequences of time, a rare thing these days, we imagined ourselves free—

...

Evidence—the collection in one place, these shelves, of an unquantifiable number of dictionaries (for example) plainly signals a form of despair. For after having stubbornly searched in one, two, three, fifteen of them, a *single, same* (*unfindable*) thing, one must (ought to) submit to the evidence that none hold the solicited thing, that the sought after thing does not exist. They all seem to signal the despair (stubbornness) of the person (me, as it happens)

who insists on *desiring* this obviously *absent* thing. Absent
for having perhaps never existed. A word—

...

—No, you see. I simply don't feel like it. I want, I mean—

...

: as if the destruction of self had already taken place so that
the other is preserved or *to preserve a sign borne through the
dark.* (Blanchot, *Celan*)

...

—clinging to one another, I could taste his death deep in
my body. His own detached from all of its bearings, having
turned to sadness, barely risen from the previous year, a
single same sadness before day, that made me into the
threshold of death and impossibility. Being and been, like
that, the window gaping, as though nothing had happened.
There was nothing, and this very nothing was examining us.

...

Touch so as not to have to touch, and what's more. Driven
into an abyss, for the abyss too is touch, and rupture and

breach and desire and amnesia. I must learn not to say: *I want*—

...

The very last photograph caught my immediate attention, it was only after having looked more closely that I was able to confirm that it was indeed Lyon, a city that marked my youth. I retain a horror of it, but the architecture of the old city stayed with me just the same; these astonishingly subdued seepages of remembering that sometimes catch one in the memorial abyss.

...

It is because of this desire for a silence other than silence such as it became intelligible that the sounds of others—*the other sounds*—imposed themselves with such violence. The volatile body wants nothing to do with it and imbibes it nonetheless—perhaps even willingly.

...

I grant myself reprieve from the *silent e*. Is this to dispense myself of silence or plunge more deeply into it. It isn't a form of *neutralisation* (Sarraute), nor of masculinisation, nor even of emasculation, but a kind of stripping bare which the body needs to breathe—*outside* the binary field that requires that one erase the other, or inversely. One being the other, the other barely recognisable in the one, is there not a logic of desistance that might grant silence its shattering? Rob the mire of its glare and make the remaining I, the remains of a mute self (not necessarily neutered), who agrees to speak, belie itself, deduce, *otherwise*?

...

It is still possible to believe in the lure of arrival. In the redemption of History. In the resulting plenitude. In our full participation. In the place, henceforth unoccupied, that awaits. In the sensuality of speech. The fervour of the caress. In the expanse of language, the expression attached to it. In other words, in the freedom that has always promised and denied always, but for which we are responsible, despite ourselves, and always, to seize upon—

...

Disfigurement—Disfigurement rests on the idea that looking does not see itself. To say what was or what will be incapacitates the present, the presentiment of that which leads in any direction from the place, where I am, would be. Where I was, might have been. (Which suggests that there is (may be) an *a priori* self, a singular place, a single and unique trajectory that isn't shattered. The I of which I speak is, might be, the shard, itself broken and fallen back upon its own shattered streets). To say *I* assumes the disentanglement, the dislodging, of all the times and all the bodies caught there, of all the languages exhausted by telling and retelling. (Re. filiation). It might therefore be preferable to make no allusion to the place occupied by a name, and rather to erase it. Erase the name of the self, the name of the name that is an armature of the self whose whole life (the life of the self) will be spent trying to come undone. Disfigurement also requires that looking have no desire to know if this knowing does not respond to the need of an other who catches one looking in a mirror. This knowing is perhaps equivalent to a form of flight in order to install oneself elsewhere in one's I, an I that doesn't wait, awaits no one. For example: She expected something from me and the thing was insufficient: disfigured. Insufficiency of the name to carry the self and of the self melted into the mirror offered as a trap. They are several and then they are many. Disfigurement rests on the idea that the painter Rothko attributed to it, that is the injunction to mutilate the figure for history had disavowed it with sufficiency. There was in the place of history a mutilation. Re. Giacometti, Eva Hesse, even Claude Cahun despite the misunderstandings. What Chillida hoped for perhaps from his Casa del Olvido. The over-fill of memory assumed by the over-fill of emptiness, strangely peaceful, or else strangulated, the silence that exhumes interiority and there defends the presence of an outside. Me, I was on my way in. Only then did I go out, alleviated, stricken.

...

In *La langue de l'autre*, Abdelkébir Khatibi's bibliography makes this distinction: Littérature, Essais—this is tolerable. His Œuvres are nonetheless divided into—1, Romans et Essais; 2, Poésie de l'aimance; 3, Essais—which is of much less interest. I think that if it were one day required of me to publish a *(in)complete works*, if, like Nathalie Sarraute, I reached the age of 98 and that such a possibility were granted me, to make my own selections, my oeuvre would consist only of torn out pages.

...

There are letters accumulating at the edge of me and I realise this is not the time to write or to send them as you are taken with so many other things, and I haven't the mettle either, I think, for unanswered missives. Just this then, to say from a space we seldom get to much these days in our conversations that it is simply suspended, the conversation, writing, our encounter, over the many miles of this city and our speaking,—

...

I would like to believe that the old face, the face from before the catastrophes, still exists, but I have some difficulty convincing myself of this; there is neither before, nor after, this distinction only serves to conceal the (dis)continuity of rupture; incessant, implacable.

...

I like this sentence: *On nous appelle*—immediately after *je t'appelle*. I first heard *je t'appelle* and sought a syntactical subterfuge in *on nous appelle*. But it wasn't that at all. It was the incursion of the real—

...

Western medicine kills illness, it doesn't heal bodies. Sometimes it kills an illness at the same time as a body. Must it consider this a success? Dead is dead.

...

Your horse too is in pain.

...

I was monsieur before having been. How strange to feel at ease in a place one has spent one's whole life fleeing.

...

Make it this far to where you aren't, upstairs a tender letter awaits and the announcement of morning: a tomorrow. Rue Drolet, one way to approach sleeping. First I am upright. Then, sideways. Between the suitcase and the bed I lose my thread, I remember nothing, and it is then that the sweetness of July invades my thinking, and I sleep in December, tearing.

...

There is this person and I must not lose sight of her. That may be a love: past the point of seeing—in the confines of seeing where one risks no longer being able to see—that.

...

How can I deny that we are very tightly bound to one another, in pain especially, a pain I am not interested in hearing them speak. And so of necessity I engage in these distances, I reject proximity. The difficulty in all of this is to recognise—and admit—that I don't want it, that the one I want doesn't exist. And then to recognise that this consent doesn't repair anything; even writing is incapable of it. The *qui-vive* being the only vital possible.

...

If I had a god, I would have slit its throat a long time ago.

...

The passage Gide cites in *Les Nourritures terrestres* from

Hippolyte Taine's *Littérature anglaise* (1863) is a collage of strophes from both "The Wanderer" and "The Exile's Complaint;" Gide only made note of the latter in his footnote. A curiosity exists in this passage in the form of a line, identifiable in neither Sharon Turner's translation of the "Complaint" (sometimes called "Song"), nor in H. Van Laun's English translation of Taine's tome (which, rather than retranslate Taine's translation back into English, thus multiplying the readings of the old text, resorts to Turner's translation, avoiding the curiosity specific to Taine's rendering). The translations are quite liberal; there are few "equivalences" to draw, and the omissions are quite flagrant. Even Gide's ellipses gesture toward expressions of love interpretable as homosexual, which operate in the *Fruits* as spectres of a (forbidden?) text. In his notes, Taine cites as his source, the *Codex exoniensis*. It is this version that the current translation reproduces, opting for an echoic transmission of reading, i.e. Gide reading Taine reading the *Codex*. Without Ch.'s assistance, I would not have been able to muddle my way through this labyrinth of versions.

...

Fin de siècle—Lyon, midnight, the mother's mother dies at the age of one hundred, on the birthday of the daughter, who has just turned sixty-three. I tabulate the wars once again: the Rif, Vichy, the Algerian war; pregnancies: thirteen, including at least three abortions, one miscarriage and a bartered child; husbands: Mordékaï, Simon, Joseph;

dead children: Claude and another whose name is unknown to me; countries: Morocco, Algeria, France; languages: Spanish, Arabic, Hebrew, French. Her body will be wrapped in a white sheet and put in the earth. Five of her children— all but the mother alerted in a fourth country on another continent, on her birthday, as well as an incapacitated son—will attend the funeral. I mean that they'll wrestle over the grave before dispersing.

...

At la Part-Dieu, a cretin stole her teeth.

...

Death apparent: a century of turpitude grafts itself onto the face, inscribing in each of its lines an unenvisageable hardness.

...

Even after having prepared an African stew and a Moroccan spread this evening, I've had enough of the disturbances of the past. F. is better off. At least she has something to push against.

...

A madness embedded in language and which almost always goes unnoticed.

...

What day is it? Time passes, for the maples as well.

...

I collect small pieces of tracing paper that measure six square centimetres. They are pushed into the little bottles of Chinese remedies I take. After a year and a half, I have gathered a pile of some consequence. The cumulative effect of the transparency is a white opacity. This incites me to want to consider freedom as a seen thing. Its symbolic value is in its invisibility; its wager is inscribed in its stratification. As soon as a value is ascribed to freedom it gets caught in a game of elusion. It moves to avoid being caught. Stratification is under the aegis of temporality. And ourselves for wanting to stop it short.

...

Thus would the notebook of deliberations concern itself with thought subjected to the examination of its own undertakings and thinking which seeks an absence of constraint. One must see in *liberation* an act and not a fait accompli, nor a decisive, locatable situation. For there is no one place that is best suited to deliberations, nor one thought (which would be *Thought*) which is best indicated, and no calendar for this process, for it would be impossible to keep track of it. I sometimes hold it against me, that expectancy; still it escapes me. What I want is to move toward it blindly, sometimes decidedly, while considering the possibility that it is always already implanted there. Which demands that I address it frontally and obliquely, that I listen, in its own voice, one which is as much mine. It is this: *of which we are a part*. Which withholds, which escapes.

...

Scrapes.

...

Today I avoid thinking of today. Of everything that might orient this particular day that practically seals off the year such as it is conceived of in the west. So I think instead of thought itself. Is there such a thing: *thought itself?*

...

When I was living in the apartment on Winchester, I would sometimes cross paths with an older man whom I referred to as *The Little Man*. He is responsible for various tasks around the building and the other properties around the neighbourhood belonging to the same landlord. The first time we meet, it is six o'clock in the morning, the day after my having moved in; he is standing in the kitchen and excoriating my things which are clearly in the way of the cleaning he must do and which has remained undone since the previous day (the bathtub, incidentally, is still stained blue from one of his products). I quickly learn to avoid him. Over the three years spent in that apartment, he mows my garden which for him is comprised only of weeds; he pulls out the young plants I've put in the soil, judged by him to be unseemly; he rips down the vine separating us visually from the neighbour, and insults the existence of all the neighbourhood dogs. He patches his big American car with plywood. His yellowing hair resembles a bird's nest, stuffed under an old hat, and one of his legs is bent in half because of an old injury. I have difficulty situating his accent. I only know that he displeases me. The day I move out, he intercepts me to wish me well. But not without first explaining to me that he fought against the Russians at Leipzig, in the Wehrmacht. Thus do I learn that he survived the bombings of WWII that liquidated 60% of the city centre, registering 6,000 victims. He survived the arrival of the U.S. Army in 1945 and the Soviet occupation. He escaped the RDA, bringing his malevolent whispers all the way to Chicago where he is now (in my fantasy) staked out. I don't know what to make of his admission. Nor of my need to denounce him.

...

Unaddressed letter—Several months after C.'s suicide, I

receive in the mail a large envelope stuffed full of letters, without an accompanying note. I don't understand right away, for none of these letters is addressed to me; they are written in my hand, and addressed to C. It takes some time before I understand that these are returns. In the face of death, life has only itself as a reference. In 2004, the return, a sort of evacuation, consists in a small pile of unaddressed letters. I feel as though I have been called upon to eat my words—

...

Thus am I able to make a connection with the other text—ALÉA (of which we are a part)—which I have also slowly begun to work on again (at least internally). For it is difficult to envision one (the notebook) without the other (ALÉA). The tension between these two works, as well as their excesses, which enable me to reflect on them, and which enables them to reflect one another; one in relation to the other, one because of the other, despite the other; one for the other. A textual interlocutor, as it were, which may account for the writing of the second, by its presence, in order to mitigate the silence in which each is irrevocably enclosed.

...

—but I don't know about after. *After* is a notion I don't fixate on too much these days, as you can imagine.— After our telephone conversation the other day, I started over in Montréal—

...

—I'm starting to think again because it's true that I don't think enough these days, my poor glaciated mind, and I am turning over this word "after"—*after tomorrow, after all, after dinner, after which.* After, then: what travels, what obstinacies, what severities, what kindnesses, what imbecilities, will I have to face.—The candle, then, that I will light, doesn't exist yet, it's up to me to invent it, or to find it abandoned at the bottom of a drawer, along with my mind.—Where will we go? Always the same question: where—drawn over all the years to come. And after?

...

The mother's sister tries to appropriate all the effects of the deceased matriarch, unceasingly called back by the caregiver. A strange consequence of death is the way in which gifts find their way back to their givers. There is something irrevocable in this which calls up our own mortality, and possibly signals one of the impossibilities of giving.

...

A painting, a Moroccan teapot, a sewing machine.

...

You see, I have just prepared a green tea offered to me by a friend during my last passage through Montréal. I am preparing it in a small blue, Japanese teapot purchased last year on Duluth and I am drinking from a small green cup. As you can see, I am very attached to this ritual, which enables me slowly to reconstitute myself after the plunder of dreaming...

...

By some inverted logic, one must, over the course of one's life, never cease to give gifts, so as to ensure its duration.

...

Who will want to admit that the North African Israelite breathed her last breath in the company of a young Muslim woman who alone kept watch over her, hand in hand?

...

Is it possible that the injury made our encounter impossible. The encounter of one with the other.—The situation, it seems to me, is analogical with the situation of the lover's malady. In very little time, the leukaemia takes the place of the relationship, such that we relate to one another through the illness.—It's possible that the injury behaves thus. It makes itself into a wall and we erect it as a protection for the self and a barrier against each other.

...

What is nearest is destroyed (Myung Mi Kim)—I open the book at page 67, I read and that is enough for me. Then I read the whole book and find the same line on page 61 and begin to doubt myself. But here it is again on page 67.—It corresponds to what I am writing now. This may be why it is incomprehensible.—Is it the pain of proximity; the devastation of the war; of illness; of topographies wrapped in this silent, detonated line.

...

The wound inflicted in the distance bleeds nearby. (Pierre Schneider)

...

I never know whether I am in life or not. For me it isn't clear. And yet: "When you paint with grey, you have all the colours." (Vieira da Silva)

...

I told him that sometimes I am drawn between philosophy (thought, literature) and the ocean. What this might represent: living by a landscape rather than through this language that everywhere imposes distances, while sometimes slamming one thing very violently shut against another. The question isn't a simple one and solicits no answer. But I am still compelled to ask it.

...

—A surge of memory.—Good.—It's life returning to a surface.—Your vitality in those found objects again.—

...

It seems to me that this book doesn't yet exist—

...

—this, which goes without saying: that every door opens onto a corridor. That the person behind the door is always the same person. With the same imbecilic smile. And the door is always another door. And the voice is always unrecognisable. But it always says the same thing. And I have never heard this language spoken. But I know that it is hateful.

...

If need be, I insult them. I don't care. Always, I bring back the question of ethics, which they seem unconcerned by. With their well-padded armour. And their stupid statistics. And their ugly, expensive faces. And their heavy shoes. I hate them all.

...

In what is it lived? In what is a body livid?

...

What binds one person to another in anger? The anger which brings about more anger and people (all at once, it sometimes seems) for whom a white, livid rage is reserved. The anger at the mother, the lover, the friend. The agglutination of angers in the folds of the skin, through which the body runs, apprehended by the intruder deployed at the moment of dislocation, passage. Past the mother, past the bitterness, past the lover. I was the lover, him, her, drawn, and devastated. Anger is what makes love's ability to have loved, to have lived, animate. In the devastation summoned by anger (love), there is the seed that set everything off.

...

—In my fantasy, which has its share of fatality (which

amounts to a kind of betrayal) I imagine that the lovers exist already—That the only possible lovers are those who are already there.—Such that in the absence (death) of the lover, the lover is always already there.—In this fantasy, I have already, in a certain sense, lived my whole life. I have already been the lover that I shall be.—Thus: the lover is always already there.—(*You, for example.*)—I hadn't intended to make proofs of this.

...

I don't know why it hadn't occurred to me, that we would speak of this. For others it seems possible, or perhaps it is that they simply don't hear the cries released by their own bodies.

...

At the airport, each will walk through the door. Each will cross the border. Each will have a bag. Each will put down the bag to be able to embrace the other. We will embrace. We will then go together into the centre of the city. Each will open her own door.

...

If I put the lover in the book am I leading him to death. If I put the lover in the book am I bringing her back to life.

...

The question of the lover cannot be posed as a question, inflected like a question. It must speak itself, be quiet, present itself on a surface resembling that of a body, a wall, a sidewalk. A book, say, in which everything is read internally, without inflection, without excess of emotion. The emotion is already buried in the question which cannot be asked as a question. It is waiting for the body to come meet it, to wait for it, there. The emotion takes the place of the question. It buries the question of the buried emotion. As a result, the lover goes unmentioned. The lover's cry is neither smothered nor silenced. It persists, underneath. It seeks a passage.

...

—opening the door and wishing for silence, another city, or this city, alone somehow, healthy, energetic, not exhausted in the way exhaustion has become the first meaning of my existence, my person, my creaturely person, exhausted, collapsed in a forest at the foot of a tree, snow, it's snowing, or there's rain, it's spring, summer again, porch parties, noise, I am walking in the city, past the porches, alone, back and forth between the apartment and the hospital, waking in the city, falling asleep in myself, in a coma of feeling, feeling anger, not apathy, why can't I feel apathy, disturbances in the register of feeling, at the foot of the tree in a forest where I can't for the life of me smell the smell of the leaves—

...

You fold yourself over and unfold yourself and in each fold is the beginning of a translation whose language remains unknown. But the language is yours; it comes to you from outside and you go to it in the parts of you that fold and fold over holding in each fold a piece of world.

...

And the book, what has the book to answer for in this?

...

Cities for a love. With or without the presence of the body, the actualisation of desire outside of letters, language, the meeting place is another place. Far from our respective homes, our beds, our kitchens, crossing thresholds in distant places, arranging to meet on different doorsteps, speaking face to face, perhaps, as though we'd only just begun to learn to speak.

...

When it had just died my death, yours, the streams of boiling tears prevented me from seeing your faces. (Cixous)

...

Here is someone I never stopped desiring. And could never near.

...

It seems to me sometimes that the distinctions founder or collapse, and that the diff... is not always so easy to identify; and then it is a Cartesian ruse to want to denounce the distance between each thing and thus to touch it, by which I mean to denounce touch, but I'm willing to go along with the misunderstanding, we also touch touching and the distance which is itself touch.—Since I am writing to you sideways on my chair, I'm going truly to go to bed now, not on the floor, but next to the cats, in the sun, I'll go to the ocean you are tendering.

...

If I put the lover in the book am I leading her to death. If I put the lover in the book am I bringing him back to life.

...

Is the lover void in the book. The lover a void. Avoid the book. Void. The lover. You're.

...

I lose a thing. I lose it and thus do I understand that it is not mine.

...

1988: A French village. I hide in this village. The young lover hides me. He must hide the young woman in the village. (Young, she thought of herself as a woman). I only remember these words of the lover's mother: *you eat like a Jew.* Eyes wide. It's just an expression. I lose my appetite. After I am not welcome. At dinner, in the guest room. Nor on the stairs leading to the top floor, at night, the other bed. So I am hidden in a small cabin on a farm. At night, he comes. It's the same terrible dream again. The hand. Inside the body he touches it. She cries out. The cry echoes. Falls back at once. There are the tall grasses and the wind. At night in the small house, there is the wind, a cry. A memory is torn. The house, I forget, and the lover. I take the train away from that place. I tell myself that the French often have something to hide. They hide the other so as not to see that which in them ought to remain hidden.

...

Benjamin's *chips of Messianic time—splinters*—in the more recent translation, evoke for me what one might come across on a beach. The parts of a life, a self, encountered inadvertently. Strewn there, a water's edge. A tear. A removal. We are torn apart by moments. At the moment of the encounter with the torn out part of the self, of a life, by turns torn anew.

...

Erosion: a faint resistance (accompanied by a lesser need for protection), the result of which is ironically a greater freedom. Ironic, because the margin is continually narrowing. To the point of disappearing.

...

The closer we get to disappearance, the more free we are. Where is the logic that grants a freedom to presence? But presence is already the threat of disappearance. Presence by the very fact of the absence at all times proposed by the temporality that makes the body into a littoral, an act into a breath, and movement into the interruption of presence, arisen there, in itself, between a self and an other. Two hands, two words, a gust of wind.

...

How is it that grief is constitutive? That inside these shards or *chips* or *splinters* there is the sense of a body moving toward something. This too is: presence. Desire as well. How *j'existe* might come to be. In relation to you, for example. I exist. Not in you but with, near you. To be near you doesn't (categorically) result in disappearance. That too.

...

I name it the dream of the double cry. (Buber)

...

It's up to me to organise people in the many rooms. Different rooms. People of different ages, there is an unquantifiable number of beds. I leave the room and come back and the beds are full of other people. Not the right people. I call upon my superiors. I try to make myself heard, listen to me, I clutch at their legs, I make some people leave their beds to make room for those to whom these places were reserved. Impossible. There is a flood of sorts. Many incidents that I forget now. Toward the end, a priest arrives to discuss some matter. He pins a small, minuscule cross to the wall, I rail, he insults me, get rid of that, this is a secular place, we are only three now, in the room hitherto filled with people, I'm furious, he is threatening, picks me up and sprays me with a big hose, he mocks me, there are people around, nobody reacts, I'm caught like an insect, incapable of loosening his hold.

...

In the street I felt as though I was coming undone, being undone, that I couldn't stand another minute of Chicago. I saw myself putting my books in boxes, my cats in their crates, leaving this perfect study, the arrangement of this apartment, the windows and the pigeons, equally impeccable, and going far, far away, into the sky with my things and landing elsewhere, Chicago is impossible today for the first time since coming here, so palpably impossible in the body of my pain.

...

I know this isn't the time, but I feel it today so deeply in my body and for the first time since this all started so tangibly that I cannot continue like this, no, not, no. My skin is in shreds and the city is coming away from me.

...

I would like for you to take my photograph with your wide-angle lens.

...

I wait twenty minutes for a bus (Addison) that doesn't run at night, I take the train into the Loop telling myself the transfer will be easier at Jackson, a man stands between me and the corridor leading from the red line to the blue line, I wait thirty minutes on the platform, at night the trains are running on a single track (I didn't know), had to disembark half-way (Chicago) to board another train, finally made it to my neighbourhood (Logan Square), I take a bus (Diversey) westward (Harlem) instead of eastward (Nature Museum) which takes me several blocks further away from my door and must then retrace my steps after realising my mistake (at every street corner I anticipate gunfire). This morning I think that I am lucky to have slept in my own bed which was in the apartment behind the door to the left on the third floor despite this city's attempts at reorganising everything. None of this takes place in a book, or in a dream.

...

To the lost letters of the *Notebook of Discord*, I would add: an old map of Paris slid discreetly into a roll of Japanese paper you bought on a trip to Chicago. Upon your return to New York, you were to have fallen upon it. But your separation from your lover led you to abandon the Japanese paper that held my secret. Much later, you mourned this unaccomplished gift, me, in the place of this misplacement, you will nonetheless have: city.

...

Joan of Arc, why not. But with this distinction: I set fire to my own pyre.

...

The body is approximate. It hasn't yet been able to occupy its own place. Language incoheres, the material body as well. Aftershock: réplique—

...

And I have thought that if this ends abruptly, if there is an end that brings about a death, I will disappear. I have thought this maybe calculated it. I will stop talking to people. I will have to. I will go out and come into this apartment, travel sometimes, stop talking. I will stop talking. For weeks maybe months maybe years. I have thought this often, that I could not bear, could not stand the sympathy of people. I will not want it. Already at times I do not want it. I distrust it. It is so desperate. The desire to cover something over when it is so raw it secretes. So raw it secretes. Such that the secretion is all there is. There is no covering it over.

...

J. M.: Is today Sunday? Right. Tomorrow I'll order the hour-glass.

...

I tell myself that each our disastered body opens a way through the debris of lost or stolen architectures to the place where we are: in pieces.

...

It is possible that the letters take the form of our bodies for a time, or else the bodies, our letters.

...

If you happen upon me in the city, will you tell me where I am?

...

We tell one another the things that we want and they are the things that we do, that we have together at the same time as we want them, as we claim to want them.

...

For example, I see Marie Dorval arriving unannounced at George Sand's at midnight. Sand calls her and she comes without hesitation. I imagine myself in the place of George Sand on the one condition that Sand is somebody else.

...

I imagined that those vessels were our bodies, irretrievable, broken, in other words a form given to a world.

...

And if you sent me uninscribed letters, I would open them, I would read them anyway.—I would know how to read you outside of language, far from the structures, the mechanisms of language.—I would know that the body will have taken its place, against language, and that it has no need for writing or speaking.—

...

In the end I attached desire in my mind to illness. I had turned my weaknesses into a reasoning that contradicted desire, certain forms of desire. I made it into a conviction. It was probably necessary for a time but that time must end, must put an end to itself, is coming to an end. It was simply a conviction that was moderated by fear, the fear of collapse instead of overcoming collapse, or accepting collapse as a movement through collapse in order to touch a greater force. That it had been necessary to make a distinction between the care of the self and the enclosure of the self. That it was easy to confuse places. And that I never thought desire would bring me closer to a stronger self, but would simply

bring about the simple reiteration of collapse again and...
again.—Now I see that these two modes of reasoning are
false. That retrenchment is not desirable, no more than the
frenetic course against the flanks of mountains. That each
of these things—doorsteps, mountainsides, hibernation
and collapse, surges—, comprise this thing called vitality.
I knew it but had convinced myself that this vitality would
one day end up killing me.—

...

Dream with me of birds tonight.

...

Against a tragedy, people try to love one another, sorrow
overexcites them, they laugh too hard and destroy one
another for the simple reason that they are alive, and
defenceless.

...

I spilled tea on your yesterday letter.

...

—I tried several times today but couldn't, twice only, as

we were leaving the forest.—It was because of the distance from the woods or the proximity to your house, I can't say.—Thinking such as I disallow myself to do, I often arrive at a refusal: a categorical refusal of [...]—I feel this refusal and wonder whether it is right for me to [...].—I can decide nothing for after, after will make its own decisions, but the decisions all seem to want to be made.—The city has already ceased to exist. My language is shutting down. My hands want only to touch paper. Nothing but that.— Must I admit it to you? Please keep this for me.—Thank you for this day, the woods and the river, this unhabitual snow, and you of course, Love.—

...

Approximations—We are sitting together in a bathtub. The bathtub is empty, there are us, in our clothes. Your head is bent, you tell me something unexpected. After, in another room you repeat it to me. I am on the bed, you are next to the wardrobe. People pass by. You are wearing a blue sweater, I am moved by your hair. It's because of this dream that the other parts of sleep are bearable.

...

Expectations of a survivor: to console the living, those who remain, make a way for them through their sorrow. Forget it.

...

The relic proposes to be reassuring. It is both living and defunct. The assurance that what dies will survive its death, that the present will carry the evidence of this, evincing its disappearance.

...

I am not the oracle.

...

Under the weight of emotion, I feel nothing.

...

Very small voice. Very open face, sad eyes, gentle. So tiny in my arms. This morning remembering this, writing this, I am so sad. A sadness that may perhaps kill a person.

...

It is a room; it is the space of the world.

...

When you say: I am your witness. It is something else.

And I think of my sister, at nine, twenty-five, thirty-two, thirty-five, and how through everything, I have been able to talk to her, and I wonder why that is, and whether it is because our pact is foremost outside of language and uncontaminated by memory, even though the memory did come after.

...

M.: Between the airport and the city. I will tell you. A heart like a bird: yours.

...

Freedom does not exist outside of the constraints imposed by the fragility of the body. It is precisely through this fragility that freedom passes.

...

Tomorrow, déjà. Now we can say of Monday: tomorrow.

...

This is the residual letter, the letter that comes after the declaration of sleep, like the declaration of goods at the border, after sleep in a body that isn't capable of sleep, attentive to the suffocation of another city, attentive to the grief that doesn't come. Sleep like an injunction imposed on the body that the body rejects, wants, denies itself. The laws of sleep which it (dis)obeys.

...

I wanted more, again. Your drawings. I wanted a drawing like that on a book I hadn't yet written.

...

Train, airport, bus, café, museum.—This is no map, isn't even mapable or situatable. That it is possible to say of a day a single day or of a city a single city. Or of a love, a love alone.

...

Le Corbusier's architecture is adulated; this is no reason not to be suspicious of it.

...

When a person very close to us is dying, there is (we dimly apprehend) something in the months to come that— much as we should have liked to share it with him—could happen only through his absence. We greet him, at the last, in a language that he already no longer understands. (Walter Benjamin)

...

Last night I dreamt that we both had leukaemia, he and I. I am trying to remember now. A subway car. A room. No intimacy. The same people in different places. People I recognise. A lover, possibly. I don't recognise her, but in the dream, yes. A danger thereabout, an emergency. Why am I not receiving a treatment. No, that's not it, we were both in dentist chairs in the middle of an airport, a very dense hall, and everything was going well until I understood that I was about to be perforated for a transfusion, and why would I consent to such a thing, I'd hardly thought about it and it seemed to contradict all of my convictions. That's what must have woken me.—It's no wonder I wake every morning a derelict.

...

Miss-remembered. Somebody, regarding me, related by A.: Remember, you invited me to read with that French girl/ woman who wrote a text in which she claims to be a man. (The book was green if I remember correctly).

...

Peaches. The most precarious fruit of the season.

...

I have sat in the morning in my garden in Guelph. At dusk in the snow. On my sister's back porch on Empire and before that on Boulton.—In my parents' garden.—The garden in Caluire.—The garden on Winchester.—The provisional garden in Antibes.—Very briefly the garden on Colombine, before my neighbour's threats, and the garden on Connaught, an abundance of Chinese lanterns.—There must be other gardens I am forgetting—There were no gardens in Banff or Norwich.—A farm is not a garden. (Devon)

...

By transposing these objects in my imagination, as far as this room, I also catch a glimpse of departure. Terrorised by the possibility of this death and tearing myself from every scrap of my own existence that might evoke this time in my life. This, I suppose, is an instance of rushing ahead into every impassible wall, every hard surface, every aspect of breaking.—The fears all rise together, and they are deafening, cruel and disorienting. Maybe this is another form of seasickness, maybe I am in your sea wreck—but the sea hasn't drained yet, is still draining.—I miss you from these many degrees of silence.

...

Someone carries a door through a door.

...

Physalis alkekengi: Bladder cherry, Chinese lantern, Japanese lantern, Winter cherry, Cape gooseberry, hōzuki, in Japanese.

...

(Apparently the blasts in the blood may be indicative of the body ridding itself of the cancer; I wondered whether this was a joke. Apparently, too, my chest just caved in, the walls of my heart just disintegrated, my pelvis shattered and my hips fell out. The body I describe cannot be mine and this is not my body to tell it to or to speak from but there is something coming out of it that is unheard of.)

...

How many obliterative forms to a day, to a week, a life? What is a life, I mean in duration? I think the conjecture of future dwellings is attached, at least in part, to a fantasy of *be-coming* which probably doesn't exist. One way of undoing the actuality of this hell is through the concoction of different structures, different modes of life, different relational forms. The wish for an other thing, itself already a fiction.

...

Derelict: the only legible book.

...

If I did sleep, it was with such vigilance that from inside sleeping I was aware of all the vital adjustments to the room: the agitation of the cats, the painter's sighs, the change of light, the dust settling, my discomfort.

...

—but is it worse to remember or to forget, maybe it isn't possible to sleep at the same time as one remembers if a state of mental vigilance resembles a state of remembering; it is no doubt necessary to relive this relentlessly until the shock is integrated, until the burn is only the trace of a burn and the heaving separates from the incident that provoked it.

...

, and death impossible to remember, (Inger Christensen)

...

I am in a room. In another bed. Each of us against separate walls. A house. Looking through the window I realise that we are quickly falling past the buildings from the sky directly toward the ground. We're going to crash I say. The house is an airplane in the middle of the city. We hit the ground, I brace myself, bounce off the bed, very high, and onto the ground beside the bed, losing control. He remains where he is, eyes open and then closed. I can't tell, are you okay. Is he or isn't he. He seems still alive but I can't be certain. Twice this happens. In another house, with many rooms, with A. this time, and her clothes. A third person, male, I don't remember whom. I rush there for a reason. With worry. Perhaps to tell the story of the crash, did she crash also. Then looking at my hands, going into the bathroom with both of them, saying look, it's just a small bruise, he says, and I lift my shirt. My body is covered with inky purple stains, bursts of violet on my skin.

...

I like to imagine those two small urns of light, one signal calling another, each from its respective night.

...

I have so often praised the unexpected that I forgot to take into account its more malevolent aspect—now that I am reminded of it, there isn't a minute to spare, on this very mild day, nor either this love.

...

Alchemy of pain—He asks what I will do this summer. Impossible for me to answer. I say: it depends. How am I to respond to such a question. I begin a sentence. He interrupts: I mean in general. In general dismisses the self from the quotidian, the pain in my mouth that says I don't know. In general means don't impose your pain on me, don't subject me to the trial of your trial, the emotion of your emotion, be such that I will still be intact after this our conversation. Make it such that this conversation doesn't take place,—

...

—very agitated now. See the phone, think of calling, can't call, speak, want to leave, if everything does fall to pieces, there will be nothing left, not here, not elsewhere, each in one's own ache, apart, M. in her blue, R. in her boxes, A. in her foetus, A. in her lungs, Ch. on her tundra, and me, my stupid, summary life, this magnificent infernal apartment today is just a place to keep me inside, hold me back, this ache is the ache of so many years, the mild air and the torment just like—

...

What if I dressed differently. What if I studied sea-horses

instead of philosophy. What if I wrote a philosophy of sea-horses. And what if I were unrecognizable. What if I swam out to sea. What if I became a boat. What if I carved a sculpture. What if I read the stars. What if I disposed of my vowels—

...

I'm impatient to see you, to learn your city again, where I always leave a scrap of myself.

...

Seaward, do you see?

...

M: Are you a sea-horse this evening?

...

My sea-horse has no gender. It doesn't ask this question. The question needn't be asked. Neither inside nor outside the body. It is a sea-horse and that is the beginning of every question. Every question begins with the sea-horse. It is itself a question that would like to be asked, that waits to be asked, and that asks (itself) also. It is the question and it undertakes, it envisions the question. It moves through a series of questions and accumulates them all in the form of movement, by accretion, a wave of questions, it formulates itself.

...

Once it is born, it is alone with its birth, it is without genitors, it has only its death to look forward to in the deepest waters and tiniest reaches of the ocean. That is where it writes itself into existence.

...

Yes, one pays dearly for freedom. (Hannah Arendt)

...

—I don't know how I'll sleep tonight without opening the floodgates, without releasing this desiring ache that reaches for you.

...

...one determines one's disaster on stage... (Noëlle Renaude)

...

In Euskadi, I never said farewell or good-bye, but *geroarté*—
"see you later"—my mouth borrowing that familiarity, and
propelling my body into the irresolute space of temporality.
Geroarté, causality undone, supplication set aside, I was
free to move toward the unknown, to stake that freedom
which drew the contours of a friendship that was always
postponed and never declined, of unwagered familiarity.

...

At such times it is impossible for me to speak to anyone.
A superhuman effort of explanation would be necessary in
order for this conversation to take place and every question
asked in the direction of precision would reach me as an
injury, a violence. This is how the moment covers itself over
and covers me with it. I can only stand my own anguish
despite my desire to move past it. Later, perhaps, when I'll
stumble upon the pot of narcissus on the window-sill and
remember that I'd forgotten it, a moment of distraction
may eventually enable the rest to be evacuated, but for
now, there is only enclosure.

...

...the sister, excluded from all referential kinship, from all
genealogical constraint, is free at present to rid herself of
it, in the language of her choosing.

...

I go back to that country to get closer to my hatred.

...

To be always in passing in the place of one's birth. Refuse the originary in permanence.

...

A Europe that has lost its footing.

...

Rue Rivard, a *Petit Maspero* in pieces, I pick up what is left, several pages underlined with fervour, and this question, sampled by chance while leafing through it, *Et les provocateurs...?*

...

I am relieved to no longer know myself such as I was, to have to rethink what was once obvious, despite the uncertainties this brings. I like for nothing to be decided, for nothing to be given, it seems to me an indication that real change is possible.

...

A bookseller: Are you a Spinozist?

...

Since yesterday, just like that, the dam doesn't burst, it desists, I am in a state of desistance. What comes in is much more forceful than what goes out. I couldn't say what it is. But the painter will have his way.

...

We are all a bit shaken I think, it's the times, I think, and we are its reverberations, we, in turn, who make the times shake.

...

At the Jean-Talon métro station, I cried inside the tenor's song. I closed my eyes all the way to Côte-des-Neiges.—At the exit it was raining.—The fire-fighters were at the foot of the building. The elevators were overheating.—I took the stairs to the seventh floor.—I felt so good at your place: thank you.

...

This is what I feel: that as this rain comes out of me just as it falls against me in this city there is something I haven't yet touched, or this thing is granted a vitality I have to confront. This is perhaps what is mistakenly referred to as love. Or is it love in the place of a mistake.

...

But a love is greater than the person who declares it.

...

In the city of a thousand bell towers, I'd take out the bells.

...

Incrimination of the body by illness—What can I do, I walk and wonder what I can do and how, and how far to throw myself into the incapacity of this doing. Where there's a will there is no way, whoever said that never considered the impossibility of doing despite the devouring desire of wanting-to-do that most often results in the absolute hatred of the self, hatred and the discourse of failure, of fault, of the fa ille and the flaw.

...

What death? What life?—What dearth? What livery?

...

Remains. A whole quasi-hysterical system of evacuations and unlimitable limits, for it is there, the body, porous as it is, fragile and porous, and nothing of any of this stops the eyes from tearing.

...

A day begun with its ending would be a day of absolute possibility. If, as you confirm, every eventuality attached to this day has already exhausted itself, the nothing facing you is comprised of every possible thing.

...

There is a great gash in the place of speaking. It is but pure speculation: fear, desolation, hope, exhaustion.

...

Nothing. In the other room I do nothing. I pick up. I put down. Things. Sit. Stand. Nothing.

...

This afternoon I came close to strangling a nurse, quickly, I left despite a voice inside demanding that I stay, I left telling myself, you again, with your inability to leave. At 4:30 p.m. I was in another taxi. I came running, insulted the taxis, the elevators, the doctors and blood cells of every description. I come out of there completely exhausted, a voice trailing after me saying eat, get some sleep, I almost vomited in the taxi on the way home, it's my whole life collapsing, and his, ours replete with all its faults, our difficulties and desistances, crude, less crude, from our respective fragilities, our incomprehensible suffering, blindly, it always leads to the nothingness of our days, imminent nothingness of stateless lovers, infirm, desperately loving, avid for a love, lived, livid—

...

I can't die, he said. I have yet to make a study of the trace left by my tears on this tissue.

...

Sooner or later we arrive at love. All that time spent in favour of misunderstanding. Now that we are beginning to understand, time is running out.

...

I can't tell the difference between a dream and not a dream.
The gravity is the same.

...

I was wrong regarding—*after*. Everything I said is wrong, a
very great miscalculation. It is already *after* and it isn't as
I had imagined it. *After*, which says nothing of *before*, and
encloses itself in an un(re)solvable present.

...

At night I lie on my stomach so as not to vomit, I want to
extract that death from him, smother it, I can no longer
say of myself that I am mad, it's something else now,
it's nothing.

...

Will you? I'd like to arrive severally, surround myself with
you as I walk through the door.—And then flee into the
streets of Montréal. Find a city square and imbibe all of its
electricity.—Unbearable, I say, but one still walks through
the door. Always the same door and never the same.—A
door over and over.—A liberally expectant stranding.

...

I don't know what to say or do either. I often do laundry and I wash the dishes. Some days I stand in the middle of the room and I repress the cry that wants to come out of me. I lie down and I get up. I sleep and I don't sleep. I fold back the city. I empty the place of the people.—In your city there is a new book with my name on it. I know nothing of it.

...

The quotidian assumes the form of a death. I make the bed and blood pools by the bed. My eyes are calling this blood. With and without the dream there is the death-bed. I curl up under the bloody sheets, my head on the pillow. I say nothing of this. I don't tell.

...

In the painter's studio, the painter sits down.

...

Montaigne wanted to die on horseback, a marvellous death without cover. (Hélène Cixous)

...

A marvellous death without you.

...

Me too I would like to be strangely free.

...

I draw out a dry and disconsolate orgasm. To bring us obstinately back to life. To make emptiness into the dwelling—the immoderation—of unsubdued vitalities. I tell myself that if I lean into the place where they spin off, I'll catch one in flight, I'll return those freedoms.

...

In 2009, after having been saved by a donkey sanctuary not far from Ottawa, there lived a donkey named Juno. Her (human) guardians neglected to feed her, and beat her canonically with a shovel.

...

Bifurcations—Between the hospital room and the wooden table, I catch myself on the way to the painter's studio. The service on the El is interrupted, I have to take a bus. The 66 goes across Chicago to California, where I would normally take the 52 bus home. It's raining, I feel like walking. At Thomas, I enter into a little nursery and emerge with a yucca on my back. There are several miles left to walk. I cross Humboldt Park, stop to greet the ducks and the geese in the lagoon gorged with the detritus of human animals (syringes, excrement, newspapers, etc.) and make a small detour to water the plants and pick up a drawing at the studio. I place the drawing in a bag I carry against my chest so as not to dirty it with the soil from the yucca, nor inflict the rainwater, the city dirt on it. What is the point of this narrative other than to bring movement back to this closed body, to call presence back once more to the city and the one who went missing.

...

Sometimes it's hard for me here. The houses look like cages, the city like the end of the world. Last night I was saying to D. that when I collapse in Chicago, the city catches me. But when I collapse here, Montréal collapses too; we are too similar.—I really must shower now. It's ten thirty.

...

Montréal, 2007–2009: I behave like a squirrel. I leave traces of myself all over: at C.'s, a box of cereal, in I.'s apartment an Italian shampoo and a lavender soap, and at F.'s a fennel toothpaste. As though to ensure myself of a future that seems presently improbable. If it happened that someone ate my cereal, washed with my shampoo and used my toothpaste, I would at least have the impression of having existed by proxy.

...

I love. I hurt. I love and I hurt. And this love that sometimes takes up all the room is indecent in the face of this vile vitality, touch and painfully beautiful. I often said friendship instead of love. Often the opposite as well. The truth is I think that I was unable to tell the difference.—Tonight I felt this: love. I understood in my body that I existed intimately in this place and I understood—precariously—that it was necessarily the place of an evasion and I was angry at myself for being so cowardly and incapacitated by that which was offering itself to me.—

...

I am loyal to love, without being loyal to an idea of loyalty.

...

J.M.: I miss you, and your cities. You'll bring them back to me.

...

In the sick-room the patient is lying down, debilitated by fear, helpless. I stand before the sliding glass door that opens onto a balcony and nothing, where a towering thug is trying to infiltrate the room and attack the patient. I intervene, terrorised, the first thug is replaced by another, just as fierce, I can't stop them from coming through the door, I had been sleeping in the next room, now I'm surrounded by a crowd of believers who are inflicting their prayer on me, at the same time as the thug is inflicting his mounting force, his thundering voice, he shakes the door, threats of massacre, I shout, my voice stays caught in my throat, the patient twists in his bed, I wrest myself from the dream, panting.—In the taxi that rushes at 4 a.m. from rue Drolet to the airport I want not to understand: death in the form of a felon.

...

Going, coming, returning, surviving. Obscenities.

...

What indecency led me to move from the second to the third person singular. Your singularity didn't deserve to be absorbed into the narrative of an unnamed other. Narrative will spare us nothing. Not that which addresses, nor that which suppresses, despises the fact of existing. I exist. You exist. We recompose ourselves from sentence to sentence, which unravel despite the days closed over the world.

...

I was so happy for our convergence, your presence yesterday, and touch. My body is more unmoored than ever, and fragile, so fragile.—I thought that if D. had kissed my open mouth with his I would perhaps have lost myself there forever. And then I wondered: but what is a kiss. Have I ever known and what body is that.

...

I think that it is also a strength to go toward what one desires. To take those kisses, to want them and to have them.

...

All is "well." "Well" means that no one is dead (yet) but that my dreams are unbearable. The nurses can't locate a vein for the I.V., and so of course the doctor accuses the patient of wanting to keep his hands and wrists free.— Every time I cross the border, I lose my place.

...

You divine me.

...

The fantasy of our mended bodies is envisageable precisely because it cannot be realised.

...

Since photography can only be an event of light, without a subject (and that is when it most resembles photography), I would like one day to embark upon a narrative that would be nothing but an event of writing, without a story, and without boredom, a real adventure. (Hervé Guibert)

...

I have always imagined myself free—free to leave. Is that freedom? If so, it has no place in an ethics of understanding, of approach, of touch, of the other envisaged (the visage of the other—*an event of light?*)

...

—Slippages, breaches in time, call us back to the order of our non-existence.

...

Writing—the first slippage.

...

Solitary inversion—Without.him, I don't write, the truth is there, he writes as much as I do by putting his tongue in my mouth like a burning irrigation that ought never to cease, and by removing it, he is the absolute co-author since writing only takes place in the lack of that tongue outside of my mouth, of that sex outside of my intestines, of that intolerable distance from the necessary twin. (Guibert)

...

He enters into the room in which I am sleeping. He sits at my feet and strokes my hip. In the street, he stays close to me, he disappears. When I speak to him he doesn't answer. We go, we come, all the toilets of the dream are overflowing and the old woman in the bog casts an evil spell on me. I take the door that nearly comes off its hinges and tumble down the stairs that fall away from the house. Each passage entails a disappearance.

...

(As I write this, a car...ostensibly...runs into another car. Squealing tires, I hear the impact, *bang*. And again, *bang*. At such times, despite myself, my mind strikes up: AMERICA.)

...

Several Silences—I despair at the fact that many (among us) circulate in increasingly girded (linguistic) circuits, that what was once unthought and visionary, contentious and risky, has transformed itself into self-important, predictable, banal, determined spaces of language. What would have happened if T. and H. had left their respective texts?—(*Twelfth Night*: Olivia to Viola (travestied)— *You are out of your text.*) That is precisely where desire circulates – *exists*. Precisely. If art smothers or excludes the possibility of desire, does it have the right to call itself art? What would art be in the absence of desire if not a thing much worse than death?

...

For whoever says death, says desire, if I am to believe Hervé Guibert. (And I want to, I want so much to believe him.)

...

VIOLA   *Good madam let me see your face.*

OLIVIA   *Have you any commission from your lord to negotiate with my face? You are now out of your text; but we will draw the curtain and show you the picture. Look you, sir, such a one I was this present. Is't not well done?* (Shakespeare)

...

If I put the lover's death in the book do I return the lover to life?

...

Requested objects—a bill, a pair of pants, a paper elephant, black thread, a ball of wax, a bloodstone necklace.

...

If I kill the book—

...

It is toward literature that I want to go, or toward death, or it's the same thing? (Guibert)

...

When I receive the news I cry very hard and then I sleep for two hours. I'm in the skies. Literally, for I have just taken off once again, this time toward a small city in the Pacific North-West called Olympia. Good or bad, the news can only be catastrophal. Upon my return there will no longer be April with its calamities. There will be May with its propensities.

...

The anastomoses seem to be in good working order despite the permanent tear.

...

In the painter's notebook I read *practicing impossibilities* instead of *practical impossibilities.* The first seems to me more reasonable, meaning more apt to be reasoned, for the practice of impossibilities necessarily entails an impossible practice: by this I mean the excession of its limits, the refutation of its arguments, for or against. There is in the enunciation of impossibility a desire—a will—to be free of it. Thus would freedom be situated against impossibility... itself.

...

The massage therapist takes each of my shoulder blades into his hands and pulls them apart. My wings thus torn off, I am able at last to fly.

...

At night I note that to rid myself of this pain I have only to plant metal spikes into my skull.

...

All this time spent (together) leaving one another. Doing without one another.

...

the kiss, nocturnal, / into a language burns the meaning they wake to, they – : (Celan)

...

I would like once more for someone to burn my tongue.

...

This is a letter for after. After R.J. To be read on a train perhaps. Between places. With the taste of him still on your tongue. Mingled with the taste of after. And you hear his voice in your sleep. And you see him on the street. And the desire is so strong that it blinds you when you are doing simple things like walking or raising your head in the city.—

...

My being-in-death.

...

I would have done better never to have learned to speak, thus would I have spared myself the odious desire to love.

...

Old Markofsky bypasses Ellis Island and chooses a name for himself by letting his finger fall by chance on a map of America. Thus do the generations to come owe their patronym, Marlin, to a city in Texas.

...

When you come to Chicago you will see that the sky occupies the space of the landscape. The sky is the *topos* of Chicago.

...

I walked for a long time after the airport. Walked and walked some more. To lighten. Never mind. Now that I am not walking anymore I am sitting down. I don't walk around the neighbourhood anymore. I don't walk through the door. I tell myself that the world is a sad place and that even this sadness wants nothing to do with me. Why would a world want a person? A world has no need for anything other than itself. With it, one disappears, "…free, as in a world." (Proust)

...

Whence this predilection for the last texts of an author? The inverse of this carefully catalogued preoccupation (I automatically take note of an author's last text and grant it, if not greater importance, a mark of distinction, as though it necessarily contained some urgency, a wisdom, a more palpable singularity, more pressing than any other text in the oeuvre in question) manifests itself at present by a fascination for the *pre-text*. *Proust contre Sainte-Beuve* for example. Must this doubled desire for extremities or the limits of an oeuvre (a life) betray a horror of the body, of vitality? That which takes the place of place, installs itself, remains, where I only desire flight, slippage... elution?

...

I don't think to call. I turn in circles. I forget my world.— Thank you for remembering me. Sometimes I think that I must be dead already.

...

… dead in the once-already.

...

After all this coming and going, two days without moving, in order to gather movement into myself.

...

I leave the house to think of other things. I walk past an abandoned lot, my mind slightly numbed. A man ejects himself violently from a car parked right next to me that I hadn't noticed and spits on me slamming the door behind him before walking away in a rage, in the opposite direction. I lift my head in surprise; walking up Milwaukee, I'm unable to integrate this violence, or the motivation for it. (Who does he think I am?) I enter into the toilet of a cafe to wash my hand where a drop of his spit is already boring a pestilential hole.

...

Is the experience of pain preferable to the annihilation of experience? (Guibert)

...

Making a clean sweep of one's actuality.

...

Everything is permitted does not mean that nothing is forbidden. (Camus)

...

Desire to break (with) literature.

...

Gangrenous kisses: I touch with my mouth and the incident skin dilacerates. The necrosis reaches the flesh where it pleases. Say, I want to say to you, the strips inter-tear, the whole body in my mouth, I envy you, vie your vitality whereas this mortiferous flesh, *maurally*—

...

1983—Mother's deign. I drown.

...

This notebook could have been called *Notebook of refractory freedoms.*

...

There's no hurry. It comes or it doesn't. Some survive for a time.

...

—Love is a humiliation.

...

The principle by which one's freedom is situated in the relentlessly postponed relation is disavowed by the reversal of the situation: free is the one who is vertiginously placeless. Free is the one who, in vertigo, falls where one is not; in other words what doesn't exist—has no there. (If being is necessarily there, free, one is nowhere without one's ties.)

...

The pigeons have disappeared from the sky. I note these days without surprise (why without surprise) that the birds fly into the wall of this building, at the height of the third floor windows. Small black masses escaped from the airs that disappear into the brickwork. They must have exchanged one roof (visible from here) for another (this one), but for me it is a suicide, of the birds and the sky.

...

At the garden centre, I exchange the pot of forget-me-nots for a packet of seeds. Life is a long time coming. Might this be one way also to slow death? For within each of these seeds death is wrapped in burgeoning, it erupts, it bursts, it doesn't announce itself. It burns all the steps.

...

J.1 explains to me that it's here (Chicago) that J.2 became J.2. The logic of this nonetheless obvious observation escapes me immediately. Panicking, I wonder where I might have become myself if the equation Place + Being = Self. For I cannot attribute to a single place the becoming-me which I would ostensibly have been granted, and upon which my self would have depended, my self being comprised of shards, of shrapnel, of splinters driven into the soil of three continents at least (hanged, so to speak, from their trees) and out of which I have spent my life trying to extract myself.

...

Vague: vagrant.

...

Now that I've decided not to travel this summer I'm thinking of travelling this summer.—What do you want... (dispossession, ever and again).

...

F: I don't want to cause you pain.

N: But I am im*pain*etrable.

...

Pain is without belonging, without ties, without origin. It is in time, it has no coordinates. Pain is an instance.

...

There is this which I am not telling you. I don't tell it to you because it has no cause to be said. The saying itself is an impasse. I am the passage and the impasse. As soon as I unblock (it) I (it) doesn't pass. Unblocking as a condition of the blocked passage. In this sense, the passage (of speaking) is by definition unspeakable (blocked). It is passed out.

...

Encasement—It is difficult for me to continue to do things for myself that are not at the same time against me. And to absorb the brutality of the course (the corpse?) of actual time (to absorb, as in a blow, but I also like the way the French for absorb, *encaisser*, calls up the English encase, to enclose, literally to put into a case, a much more rare acception in French, but just, appropriate one might say by taking it upon oneself). I take it upon me. J'encaisse.

...

Exutory—At the edge of the lake the sobbing shakes the foundations. The house falls to pieces, the whole neighbourhood is drawn toward the shore, including the people, the trees and the firmament. You hold me to my chair and against you, trembling, tears, the blood rises in my throat, you say nothing, sit me down and the pain that provokes the stampede, there remains you, then me, in your arms, and the wooden chair—

...

This magnificent water of Lake Michigan redesigns everyday the shore and we, human beings, struggle stupidly against its current. The children were running in the sand, digging holes and carrying water back in their hands, I glimpsed myself small and I understood that I was already dead, unremittingly dead, living in the death of dying lives.

...

... I think I've found a way to live (with) this horror, I wrote a brief text for this book that delivers me (nor it) from nothing, but suffers its presence haunted by the present.

...

Schist— Believe me, I have no faith in archives, in the embalming frenzy that seduces this actuality, the cataloguing by anticipation of one's personal effects, of one's ground and one's artifice, I don't believe in the interment of living life and its adjoining death, in the encasement of sighs, the spectacle of the joists of fallen dwellings. The archive is against life, against what breathes, it steals from time its proximity while busying itself with untangling bodies from their torments, from their struggles and throes, from their agonistic phantasm, like a book, I tell you, and I incite myself, in counterpart, to defend against the agonic knot. I open and I see, I apprehend, that which of me is not mine and not being (of) me address myself a catastrophal retort— This book is not of the present, if the present wills itself as impervious and impainetrable. But if the present is a shard among other presents, aching and unconstitutable, and in a state of perpetual disintegration, if a drowning of ten or forty years ago can provoke a seism now, the now of many times over, I can admit to the reiteration of a multiplicitous book which has earned its divided death, and it is dead that I bequeath it, in deed and in detriment: book, brooked.

...

Yesterday submerged by another wave of terror, I come out of sleep broken, nothing in this pleases me, I am afraid, helpless, this war is killing me slowly, and every day I must remember that it isn't my war but a devastated field onto which I may inadvertently have stumbled, and it is unawares that every day I survey the area, precisely where the borders have been closed again and the bridges have all been blow to pieces.

...

...And so of course, despite having decided not to travel this summer, I catch myself looking at plane tickets to Montréal, this summer I'll have no age, the time of my thirty and eighty years is now, I am dying of ambient death and want to shake this terrible despotic disposition... never mind, tell me how you are living these days, take me out of my stupidity from there your place of passage. Baci. Nathanaël—

...

This is but one possible digression. I could also have made mention of the West Bank and the new technologies designed in this country that introduce death camps into individual bodies by way of metal particulate that burn people up from inside. Surely the designers of this weaponry consulted books in libraries.— If it were possible for what is called, what calls itself "poetry," to be wrested from the economies that seek to contain it, domesticate it, order and *diffuse* it (the French *diffuser* is to distribute, and the English homonym, *defuse*, treats it like a bomb) then it might be equally possible for it to fulfill its testimonial imperative, that is, for it to be present, as testimony, to be accountable, as accountability, through and to language, outside of whatever might want to bind it; testimony itself being catastrophal, the bind here, I am not alone in proposing, is that testimony resides inside catastrophe itself. Such that the book, in order to be read, must be on the verge of burning. And the building that will attempt to house it, already in flames. Thus, do I concur with Jacques Derrida, in *Was ist Dichtung*, when he orders "you will have had to disable memory, disarm culture, know how to forget knowledge, set fire to the library of poetics." That it is incumbent upon our memories to be forgetful, upon our buildings to burn to the ground and upon our languages to admit defeat, to allow for these (im)possibilities.—For even the library, whose purported aim is to preserve these populations of writings, to protect them from the inclemencies of war, fashionability and poor taste—but these protections are not without some relation to a protectorate, which might be the decidedly bordered territories of poetry, of thought. Such that the question for me becomes a very simple architectural one, it is the question of the doorway, in French, *l'embrasure*, with its attendant gesturings toward desire. Who is standing at this door? Who opens or closes it. And what might become of this threshold if we were to cross it, to cross it out?

...

Crabs remember being hurt. (*Harper's*)

...

What do you think you want? Will me.

...

In the *Harper's* index yesterday, I read this: "Crabs remember being hurt." Immediately, it answers every question, all the despair and the desire at the same time. Finally this memory, even obliterated (Nietzsche's memory?), might be a memory of pain, and without this pain it would not be possible to live (because *remember* is also *re-membering*), while life, with its pain, is unliveable (because pain covers life over, memorially). I don't know whether to call this suffering. This would moralise the wound. And yet, sutured, gaping or pustulent, the wound has no interest in morality. It opens. We enter it. Only then is it (up to) us.

...

For every man or animal fears, at this hour at which man walks at the same level as the animal and where every animal walks at the same level as every man, it isn't suffering, for suffering is measurable, and the capacity to inflict and to tolerate suffering is measurable; what he fears more than anything is the strangeness of suffering, and being led to endure a suffering that isn't entirely familiar. (Koltès)

...

(...these fissures are implanted in the concrete structures that surround us, somewhat in the way that madness is implanted in reason, and vice versa. It is unavoidable, and if we were less intent on enclosure, the excesses would be less disorienting. Rational spaces only exacerbate the so-called maddened spaces, but of course we would have to come to an agreement as to a meaning to attribute to these terms, reason and madness, for they are perhaps not as contrary or refutable as they may at first appear to be.)

...

Each is free to live out madness as seems unfit.

...

Despite my predilection for the masculinity of this city, I can't take its sentences and verdicts anymore and find myself asking questions I thought I'd resolved a long time ago, as to those behaviours considered acceptable and those deemed to be suspect, as to oppressive discourses, it's all very exhausting. But good nonetheless, because it brings me back to my pain, and my pain to my language where

I am able to speak it against and despite the discourses of enclosure and sequestration.

...

I have the dream in which you love me.

...

Next I have the dream in which my gums are shredded, and my mouth is not a mouth but a minefield.

...

She believes the son will save her. She opens the door to greet him before he even exists. She yields her place to the son. She has nothing to say. She shouts, she cries, sometimes she whimpers in her sleep. With no knowledge of the existence of the son, the daughters secure from the mother the unique permission which is that of waiting like she does, in their gut. Of installing in their guts the expectancy of the son. The occupation is complete. The expectancy is deliberate. It precedes all of these existences. What isn't said is the silence of the father. Pained, sometimes exasperated. Once only, he will pronounce a judgement which will dispense him of the judgments to come. His deliberation, like the expectancy of the mother and the daughters, will be complete.

...

Just how far is literature's fault literature itself.

...

Nous sommes finis. There it is. The unconjugatable verb, poorly conjugated. *I am finished.*—Please forgive me, everything that passes through me now is bad.

...

It would have been necessary for our literatures to be able to survive themselves.—But to survive, is first to die, and to die, is to kill. *Unavowably.*

...

A disease is ours only from the moment we are told its name, the moment when the rope is put around our neck...(Cioran)

...

These days I come upon a line in an issue of *Harper's* which repeatedly provokes a frenetic collapse—I find myself with this sentence before an unequalled truth (unrivalled, but can one say such a thing—or would it have been necessary to say: an unequal truth).

...

Existen't.

...

The relation doesn't authorise the solitary withdrawal of one cut from the other, and it is this in part which nourishes the anguish of our decisions in the quotidian as well as the greater, wrenching existential questions. Existence always draws the other along, even from without our most abject, recalcitrant and rebarbative silences. The very painful I forcibly draws in a you, just as painful; there is, of course, in this, a share of will, but force also, the I that obligates itself, is obliged, to consider its own freedoms in accordance with the freedoms of others. Me facing you. Deliberated liberty.—

...

...the pleasures taper, make themselves more and more discreet, they are implanted in our infinitesimal parts, far from the pain which, it, is so vast.

...

This is an insignificant little note, a sign of the hand, a smothered signal, a hello from Chicago where summer continues not to disclose itself altogether—these middling seasons are sometimes terribly punitive and sometimes a relief, undecided as they are, and people don't leave their homes, or else they're right to stay in.

...

You lean your head against mine and say: I can hear the ocean.

...

This book, once mine, would no doubt be better served by my silence than by my little destructions, but one never really knows what is good and what is stupid and which of these deliberations infringes upon the liberties of the book, those of which one might say its.

...

Nisquiera is a very beautiful word. I will probably always prefer *mojado*. It's so sensual. The mouth that opens onto this word cannot deny the body.

...

Today marks the second market of the season. I saw T. there who is a month ahead of my sister. It all makes me terribly sad. This sun on this day of the week and the many flea markets and bouquets of flowers. How is one meant to attend to such a day?

...

Jelinek: I have no idea. It's possible that, like me, you will be very interested at the start and then become very quickly bored. It's a novel and novels (I mean *contemporary* novels) are boring and predictable, not the least bit when they go out of their way not to be.

...

The question: *what's the difference?* pursues me. In other words, where is my I-me, what of Nathanaël, Stéphane sometimes, I don't recognise us anymore, do not recognise. A friend sometimes begins her sentences (because we've known one another for a long time), with "but you are" and now I tell her that it is not, is no longer, true, there is no "me" as there was once a "me," nor this "is" away from a form of hatred, directed at myself, the place precisely where I disappear (inside the pain of the other? that I make mine, my pain, a pain that comes to me from outside and in, a pain past me), in the end these itineraries are of no interest and the gasping that strews the "it isn't me," how, under such circumstances is one meant to say to someone you, at the top of one's lungs, striking the infinitude of a world that is so terribly closed.

...

The border between here and there seems to be enclosed in my body which has never crossed the Mediterranean to Oran where my mother was born, but I grew up surrounded by Arabophone Jews and their ferocious identification with French culture, notwithstanding their own sufferings. I have tried to disentangle these contradictions far from these influences, given that I renounced all contact with my mother's family for reasons that are far too banal to go into. In my refusal of antecedence, I am nonetheless able to identify in myself several resonances that need confronting and to travel "there" without "them" grants me a certain autonomy vis-à-vis the narratives that fundamentally underwrite those geographies.—It saddens me to think of this history which isn't ever far from something irrevocably broken. It is perhaps irrelevant to this conversation; but it serves as evidence of the incapacitation (mine) to overcome certain existential faults and the violences they carry.

...

To leave, is not to recover.—To return is to recognise the existence of an (elusive) already...

...

... death is unthinkable. (de Beauvoir)

...

Thank you for writing. The bond between the self and the so-called world (the world calling a self? recalling a self ... oh); let us not hang ourselves from our dried umbilics, fold into the space where we escape.—Forgive my delirium, it's the heat.—I'm running late.

...

Give and forget.

...

To call emptiness to the territory is to set fire to a part of the self to return it to the part of life that got away, the spoken part, free, perhaps.

...

Se puede morir de presencias. (Alejandra Pizarnik)

...

On the first page of *La vie heureuse* I read: "I am in search of a body that will console" and I think of you and L. who, for me, is but the shadow of an idea and of the movement you've already introduced into your summer. Again. Again. The season begins, for me with this line (Bouraoui again), "Death enters into the summer." What will it be? I ask myself the same question. The possible outlets and trajectories. Whether everything must end with a wall. *Le Mur* (Sartre), imprisonment, execution. A cemetery, betrayal. Deferment. Culpability. Sartre, for me, is always far. The distances are much greater. Because of language and affect, often un(b)reachable.

...

Now I no longer know how to answer to a name. Whichever. I don't know.

...

I make efforts so as not to ask questions regarding after, the present, or before. It's probably a way of killing time.

...

...one can but translate *poorly* and take pains to do poorly, to un-do what is bequeathed, what is assumed as inheritance (acquiesced-to fetterings, even under insistent imposition), that is which word is given while taking pains to meet it where it sinks into the *sombra* of an infinitely incomplete dream. Somber reason at the heart of which is the concealed shadow.

...

Last night I dreamt that we spoke to one another. It happened very suddenly, the speaking.

...

This text is both very fragile and very hard. Impossibly hard. It doesn't breathe. It seems right for it to be inscribed in the realm of theatre. Where what is spoken is the body in all of its pieces.

...

It was no doubt the desire for a thing, a form of recognition or a place, something of me that was abandoned. I should have arranged for fear to be nothing other than fear instead of trying to enclose it. The fear that overcomes. It isn't at all enclosable. But in order to have a voice I must kill all the parts of me that are incapable of speaking.

...

I erased more than one letter, I couldn't reach the end of my thinking, I re-erased, but please know that I tried very hard, it's just that the foundation wasn't solid and I would have preferred to send you a smile or my handprint, even the collapse of my mind, anything but these strange accommodations of language.

...

I am trying not to think of my life as a disastered landscape. Riddled with craters and contrariness. For example the four years spent in Chicago could be nothing but that. One single uninterrupted catastrophe. Preceded by a number of catastrophes leading backwards to the moment of my conception. Sometimes, it's true, I have thought this, that my body is comprised of these violences alone the shock waves of which continue to reverberate such that vitality draws life from the violence out of which life is made.

...

—I would want now to be able to walk across the rail line into the park in the rain and retrieve the moment of rupture, of breach. Undo the inn and the exasperation, the stifled feelings and violent anguish, the suffocating sleep and recapture something of desire or touch, something of a shared language. Extend a hand. Say: come.— I tell myself that it's time, something of time that is excessive, and it is this much time in order to find these precise words. I am left with these stumblings, awkwardness.—I am not asking for anything. I am trying to give something back, to put something back in its place.—I strangled my voice, I tried to preserve myself out of a fear of damagings, I put distances where there were none, here as elsewhere, and now that I don't know myself or recognise my own name, I turn to look and there is nothing left. All in order to preserve a life, to still the rocking, to stop the capsizing, to find a measure for a world that seems at times to be irretrievably broken, and endlessly breakable.

...

I think of a friend who several years ago swallowed barbiturates and didn't die from it. Her stomach was pumped a day and a half later, she spent four days at the hospital waiting for her body to stop. For her suicide to actualise itself. A *posteriori*.

...

The Eyes of the Skin: "There is a strong identity between naked skin and the sensation of home; The experience of home is essentially an experience of intimate warmth. The space of warmth around a fire-place is the space of ultimate intimacy and comfort. [...] Home and the pleasure of the skin turn into a singular sensation." What Pallasmaa doesn't say is that he is granting the house ("home") an absolute significance. It is an ideal. And the house can mean, can want to mean, many other things, which are not innocent, nor nostalgic, nor pure.

...

Bachelard writes: "Always, in our dreaming, the house is a big cradle." I read this with *What Began Us* in mind and I have at the same time a violent reaction against this imaginary, I think it is too determined, privileged. The cradle is also the crypt, the tomb.

...

The sum of Pina Bausch and those chairs.

...

In two years, I lost traces of myself that I had thought impossible to lose, I learned a form of coarseness and a form of tenderness and an unbearable fragility. And letting go of some of versions of me and losing sight of others, I learned that it is as unjust to say I am as it is to say You are and as a result I wonder now interminably what it is to face a person. What it is to face a person without a face of one's own.

...

I ask only that you read the letter. I suppose that a sent letter is a letter that asks to be read.

...

A thing that resembles freedom, a freedom outside of language that finds form in language.

...

Triste cuande deseo y cuando no. Triste cuando con un cuerpo y cuando no. Triste cuando con su sonrisa y cuando no. (Pizarnik)

...

The same person dies repeatedly, we were three, one dying, many situations, some concerning a house or a washing machine, perhaps a public square, I don't know, but the death finally comes, I who await it, the death that doesn't come, and then it comes, and I watch—no, there were crowded streets, different institutions, a school and then another one, I was perhaps changing schools, an unravelling sweater, some kind of violence, a person standing in a washing machine, many people and traffic, but the death comes eventually, all the dreams entangled and interrupted, I hardly remember, just in pieces, the telephone pulls me out quickly, and also the desire no doubt not to know anything about all of this but it doesn't prevent the rapacious grief of the thing.—How am I to wake beside a person with these things projected in my head?

...

Doors are opened for me, I walk through the doors that are opened. I can do only that. Go to the place where I am expected.

...

A hermaphrodite is able to have divergent desires, none of the existing categories is occupied. That desire is determined by none of these in anticipation of anything at all.

...

Dictatorship and time. The primitive conception of life and time. Man and time, no; man, essentially as time. Therefore, man is manifestly nothing. (Imre Kertész)

...

What of those cities that give us a desire for excess, but of *something else.*

...

July—Montréal brings me back to me, puts me *face to face.* So I lose my place, I'm completely disoriented.

...

This morning before drawing the last of my things together, I took the stem of gladiola, the lily, the thistle and the daisies, and left them with the monument to the fourteen women of the Polytechnique. Just downstairs.

...

Freedom is perhaps measured by the number and variety of incognitos one can espouse...(Kertész)

...

Last night and this morning for example, overly agitated, want to slam all the doors. I keep quiet instead and tell myself that the problem isn't there, the door is not to blame.

...

J.M.: I chose painting because it was what was most difficult and most salutary. Perhaps for the same reasons that I was drawn to you.

...

If only it were possible to wake outside from sleeping in a bed, turn over and be in the damp grass, hot sun and walk in instead of having to walk out.

...

Nothing nor anyone died in my absence.

...

This morning I would like to be able to go down to the river or the sea and stretch out among the algae.

...

The mysoti seeds sprouted and have become paralysed in that embryonic form. They didn't grow and flower. It fills me with immeasurable sorrow. The possibility of these blue flowers in the blue flower-pot: forget-me-nots.— And what have they forgotten if not the vitality enclosed in each of the seeds, the suggestion of which is in each of the arrested leaves.

...

Is it a forgotten life or over-much vitality? Arrested by its own momentum?

...

Perversity of existence: not dying of the death of others.

...

Overture (*bis*): the park where we meet, standing in the rain, crying or walking in silence, sitting without speaking, doing nothing, a fire in a small house or crossing the plains.

...

Syncope: I skip over the present and fall into presentiment.

...

At present, the present, I don't know. The body is emitting faint, worrisome signals, I smother them so that they may cease.

...

I cannot afford to be a mirror. I must be as opaque as the pavement that sops up the sun, or tar, or brick, or night. Don't want to be the face of that death.

...

You call me. You want to hear my voice. I watch the telephone ring. I wonder whether I even have one. A voice.

...

By the time I gather my courage and make my way toward your city, you, like B., will already have left. Are we moving targets?

...

In the change room of a jeans store, a song is playing. The voice insists: *are you a boy or a girl?* My jeans give no answer.

...

...every "natural" death is foremost a violent death. (Claude Lanzmann)

...

Last night I understood something that I have since forgotten.

...

Of our walls, I know nothing. Of our lives either. Of suffering or cities or animals locked in cages and the unfounded mutilations of human beings. Of knowledge or cruelty of travelled distances. There are seas that are shrinking and great expanses of garbage where habitats were, the places we wander, incapably bridled to our impossible, imperfect desires.—Must we run so far?

...

There is no part of me that is not in relation with another person. It is in relation that violence is done, without even the intervention of deliberate force. Speaking is violence as well as touch and abstaining one from the other. At least symbolically. Not the violence of decapitation or disembowelment, but a violence nonetheless that arises with the world, that is in the world, with dwelling and occupation and the face, retreating and thinking. The transcendence of this violence passes through violence, on the other side of which there is violence, again.

...

And how could I have left if not before the city began to exist again, in the plenitude of its existence, which engendered me?

...

There were myself and the city. There was no one. The beaches were full. I was invisible. The children in the water, the people stretched out on their towels, the gulls, the pebbles, the shore. I kept watch.—I had the strange impression of the beginning of a farewell to Chicago [...] Thank you for this flame. Now the sky is silent. I'm thirty-nine. Dust.

...

Whether it is a pact or a bond or a promise or a neurosis or a pathology or a headlock, I think yes that there is something very powerful that pulls us toward one another. It is in soft and hard parts of the body, and the elusive parts of language, the books that catch fire and the damp, soggy ground, the unfurling of flowers in the early morning and the bank of clouds here before me, the distances that pull at our mouths when we are close to one another, hungry for more mouth and the sleep that doesn't come.

...

This is not the letter I am writing you. The letter written

from shreds of lung swollen from sobbing, from flakes of teeth after too much tension and crumbs of bone snapping in the same dream that disallows sleeping. What I come upon in the blue cloud paper, the green and blue tie, the letters, your seal, my name written out, and this offering, which chokes me back: Rovner.

...

Whether love comes as a boy with girlish limbs. (Lisa Robertson)

...

And yet the ocean doesn't break like glass.

...

What is a morning garden, yes. I can see it, feel it almost, and think of the thresholds one must cross, barefoot, cool ground, dew. Sun on a horizon.—My morning garden is entangled today. Rovner in the early hours, Outside, over and over. Very little repose in sleep. Caught now in brambles and untidy gorse, the matter of my mind, sinking into dark mud with little resistance.—Between death and abandon.—I'll walk there and back.—

...

So I may be dead because the chronology of my life is completely abolished, I penetrate its circular spirals by a thousand ways. (Lanzmann)

...

Hard breaking sleep against the porch boards, wild wind, fine rain, some sun, wind mounting, paralysis inside and out, limbs heavier and heavier, sleep deeper, dreaming more and more violent, a hell, several hells, riveted to the wood digging into my hip, and wondering is this breathing, is this death, the sleep of the unsleeping,— forgive me, I am going to walk or sleep more, pull rain from the sky, try to find something in me that responds to the world, that is not all pain or fear or devastation (your word) and feel it, even fleeting,—I'll try again and again until I can reach you, reach out past the metaphysical blows that rain hard into my brain.

...

The whole sky at my throat.

...

As long as I am dreaming I am alive. The dead don't dream. (Darwish)

...

Yes, with my whole mouth.

...

(On Altgeld yesterday, at California, I put my bare hand against the bare wood of an undressed frame house, very very old, with the bricks taken down and its structure exposed, the bare pine at the front and the dark dark weathered brown of the other planks, waiting, it is waiting to be covered up. I touched the north side of the house in three places and the east side twice, feeling its fragility, the beautiful hue underneath that is usually hidden from view and the care with which it was stripped, bare. Not thinking ahead to what damage may be done in the re-covering, but at least it is not being torn down).

...

So I stay with your ash and your burn, your *fleur de peau*.

...

Because to choose is to kill. My mother was incapable of choosing, she wanted it all. I'm like her. For my graduate studies in philosophy I chose the following subject: "Les possibles et les incompossibles dans la philosophie de Leibniz." Incompossible means that there are things that are not possible together, to elect one is to prevent the other from existing. Every choice is a murder, they are called "deciders," they are paid a very high price for it. It isn't an accident if Shoah lasts nine hours and thirty minutes. (Lanzmann)

...

The dirty story is a story that is in accord with many of our bodies, the dirt isn't always the same dirt, and the bodies are not always the same bodies. All are violent, even the redundancy of the story is violent. That more than anything.

...

N: What is the paradox, M., of the peach's hermaphroditism?

...

I walk. I would have wanted to walk very far. But it seems in this city it is not possible to walk far enough. I walk instead up and down, there and back, I come and I go.—I walk and I think of the gardens I have left. The places I have gone. The people I have walked away from.—I walk and I think of the names put on me and the names held back, the fashioning of humility from humiliation.—I walk and I wonder: what does it mean to miss a person.—I walk some more.—The thought of you comes upon me

hard and fast. I harden. I open. I am taken aback. Is this a
fear. Is this a love.—

...

We are afraid of everything that confirms the ack-
nowledgement of our dependency, afraid, that is, of sex,
love, and thought—which probably amount to the same
thing. We should like to see ourselves as free, as masters of
ourselves, at least to some degree. Yet sex and philosophy
alike are rigorous and fatal experiments in chemistry. With
a remainder of silence around them that words surround in
all directions. (Anne Dufourmantelle)

...

Why do I always choose the same wall and not the door?

...

In the evening we sit on the boulevard under the rain with
the fireflies.

...

N: You are right, about the rain, and the door.

...

What I know: that a glass of water, room temperature, with a sliver of lemon, clears the body at the start of the day.—That marinating in the sun on the porch with the Thunbergia, the mint and the lavender for fifteen minutes releases poisons from the pores, and regardless, it feels good. It softens the muscles and demands an immediacy—heat.—That the floor boards underfoot are the habitat of these cats, and my feet, and that at 6:30 there was too much noise in the street from here to the mailbox.—Then there is the present.—Will you go to the pelicans. Will you walk through a marsh and under a bridge.—

...

Your books and mine on a same shelf.

...

N: A club for hermaphrodites? But I am one and divided.

...

Strange rain yesterday in the early evening. A bright sky with dark clouds, rain falling from the sun. I sat on the Diversey brown line platform with my book in the rain, reading, waiting for the train.

...

2:16 p.m.: downstairs, a scene worthy of Beckett. Two men, one on a bicycle, the other on foot. They argue, they fight. There is shouting, it escalates, de-escalates.—My hand on the receiver…I hesitate. They must always act this way. Why involve the police. *Bitch.* This is the preferred insult of the two men who are visibly behaving like abject lovers bound to one another by rage, and I don't doubt it, economic disadvantage.—Now they are friends again. One rides off on his bicycle, the other in his car.—Now I understand that it's the only way they know how to touch. Instead of fucking, one sends the other into the bushes. Instead of caresses, one calls the other one a bitch. And instead of kisses, one knocks the other off his bicycle. Love is so complicated.

…

I lose everything. I must have left my head on a shelf three months ago with all my things, and my body busied itself reorganising my things without letting my brain know.

…

The lover who doesn't forget sometimes dies of excess, exhaustion and tension of memory—(Roland Barthes)

…

Wednesday I wake raked over by sleep, coal in a sand-pit from the night before after everyone has gone home.

...

The doctor proposes a new treatment, I plug my ears, I don't want to hear it. I abandon them to their tryst. What a strange dance, but me, I've left the building and I'm crossing the field far from the elevators and the technologies. I despise technologies and elevators and no one listens to me anyway. So for once I go to the beach. Near Harbor County, Michigan. *Harbor, harbour.*—It will thrill you to know I'm reading Nietzsche today.

...

Distinguishing between one's own volatility and the volatility of another is no easy task. Sometimes it seems that volatility is of the world and that we enter into it. How is one to meet an other through it, that's something else again. There is also the question of the world.—As for me, I'm not opposed to calm, but I don't want stagnation either, or what claims a form that isn't its own ("own"). And it's so very fluid and transmutable and I aspire to be with what is transmutable, rather than to try to fix anything at all.

...

I end/s up being nothing more than a fine wire stretched from pain to pain and strangeness to strangeness. (Nancy)

...

August—A. at Banff, and M.L. and A.G.... the beginnings of my illness, that strained fatigue, and the intervening years of movement, loss—Montréal, Norwich, Barcelona, Zarautz, Toronto, Chicago—all the things you already know. Just after our first meeting in New York, with the Slovenes in the overheated apartment in Williamsburg. Naked bodies sprawled, entwined in the large room, in heat, Manhattan visible from the window, minuscule. The lesbians in the living-room splayed over several beds, Br. in the kitchen behind the door, just outside the bathroom with the tiny sink.—August is also Antibes, the beginning death of my big dog, the blue sofa, the east end of Toronto, the small creature's strained breathing, the white of Iowa City, the returning illness—the 1st (2008), the 2nd (2007)— the shrieking fall in the green stairwell, the reddish door left ajar (2005) then closed (2008), the kiss on the dam at midnight, that time when I became (2000) a boy—

...

A quiet day, too quiet. I withdraw, very deeply, with books on the porch-garden, I don't go out. Yes I do, as far as the boulevards, but I have invested myself so much with this neighbourhood that it has become a sort of extension of *this place*, outside, yes, but barely at the periphery of this dwelling, at the bottom of the stairs, past the gate, and to the left, the paving stones that lead to Sacramento.

...

For already, I trail after me too many corpses. (Claude Cahun)

...

I let the brother in. That is the root of the problem; the problem routed to itself.

...

I miss you too. And I am missing something which likely isn't missing at all.

...

When I search in the library catalogue for *Écrits: a selection* by Lacan, the search engine asks me whether I mean *egrets, a selection*. I might do well to follow its counsel...

...

Quasi una fantasia—I did not have a Canadian or Québécois

upbringing, I don't know what it was. Sephardic Jews (pieds-noirs) transplanted from North Africa to France dogmatizing always from a moral high ground (of chosenness) and bemoaning the lost days of fraternity with "les Arabes" ("we were like brothers"), troubled narratives of rape and animal sacrifice and knifings in the public square, that's what F. had for breakfast growing up, and incidentally the other day on the phone she reiterated her fear to me as though this were an inalienable truth, get that story out of your head, how long has it been? sixty years? Her sister beating my cousins (whom I hated) and P., British, "Gentile," shaking his head wandering out of the hornet's nest saying *let's go girls* and taking us to the old port in Antibes, the water couldn't drown us fast enough, or to visit various places, Lyon or Gorges du Loup, anything not to have to deal with F.'s hysterical family, and F. too enmeshed to give herself permission to come with us, provoking all sorts of arguments with P. Later in Lyon confronted with all the same bullshit once again the most striking memory of that same sister of F.'s (who is despicable, really, gorgeous and detestable and wounded and violent and brash and unforgiveable), her most striking memory is of me at eighteen at their Shabbat table or Yom Kippour, I don't remember, pushing my chair away from the table during their prayer and she still hasn't forgiven me. And the other sister entreating me to stop causing scandals in a family that put me on weekly trial, each confiding his or her insanity to me, so many excuses not to be free of those fetters, the narratives of persecution turned inward and projected onto their own children, my one cousin masturbating her baby boy saying *but he likes it, it makes him feel good,* the whole family coming down on her like a tonne of bricks, but no one really did anything, I must have been fourteen or sixteen, I wonder today what has become of him—is he a rapist or fucked up in what other way sex-obsessed and incapable of intimacy? I don't even know him. Narratives of Jewish-not-Jewish and the Catholic convert not Jewish enough and the rest of everyone eating their ham without disturbing their judeity because it's in their blood, bloodshed, blood libel. There was also that Sonata in C# Minor and the sparrow killed by a passer-by downstairs from the apartment in the 18e, the cigarettes smoked at the far end of the garden and the fresh doughnuts on the coast. No talk of gays though and I was too male-identified to discern a desire for women, still caught up in the reenactment of the bedroom scenes with the brother from twelve onward, careening into various scenarios of sexual violence, extrapolating a philosophical real or an embodied freedom or something, and it wasn't until L., my lover of five years, that my desire was pinned to the rape of the twelve-year-old girl, but not without a hyperbolic exoneration of the brother, first-born male and prodigal son ("he found you pretty") and despite my refusals and ultimatums, really it's a wonder F. ever disowned the bastard, even if it took her almost thirty years and my abdication to do so. – Tell me, what does a man have to do for his wife to leave him on his honeymoon, this is a question I ask myself over and over, and what the hell was the bride thinking, I'd like to ask the boy some day though I needn't, *he's dead to me*, more or less, standing as he is, in the door, blocking my view of—

...

Desire begins to take shape in the margin in which demand rips away from need: (Jacques Lacan)

...

We are adrift, no?

...

Very early I elaborated a philosophy of indemnity which consisted, within a relationship, of breaking the tie attaching one to the other (attaching the *I give* to the *you take* or inversely) thus situating the (unavoidable, fiercely desired) relation at the point of the schism, the separation, the fault (line). A relation which didn't intrude on the demand for autonomy of the one who, identified to devotion, distinguished herself nonetheless from the other who gave contra-distinctly (and without indulgence).

...

A difficult passage, by that I mean the passage of a book but also of this threshold, there, the door, the porch boards, and the free fall. Or a backwards descent on all fours. I'll take my wings. It's the only possible, don't you think?

...

Yesterday I sat in the sand-box with a friend's little boy. I talked to the cats. Today in the mail, the latest issue of *Open Letter*, worse than a mirror. Tomorrow the lake. I am thinking of my time and wonder how a moment comes to be absolved of itself, how that can be, and how it is that it tends instead to bog itself down, coating the internal surfaces.

...

I would like to be able to make up my mind, whether to stop reading a continent or eating chocolate.

...

It comes so slowly, a sensation in the body which is the memory of my body in a present that escapes nomination, and touch, because it has escaped its presence.

...

M: When we first met you called out to me from a window. Your voice first.

...

They lied to us about the horse's age. (Duras)

...

When I read Duras, I hear the cry and the echo of the cry.

...

In Chicago, too, despite the rain, we walked very far, stopping by turns on the boulevards where, overcome by muteness, I said nothing, and she listened to me.

...

I forgot to tell you that the myosotis are simmering in their blue pot.

...

If the disturbance isn't internal, it is external. Both are sometimes indifferent to one another.—I am reading *L'Éden Cinéma*. The narrative of the mother and the dam. The paddy fields flooded with salt water, the children buried in mud, the dead horse, Monsieur Jo, the North China lover: "ma première prostitution."—The air is fresh, mild.—My eyes are tired, dry.—Bruised by yesterday. The violence I do myself by wanting too much too fast. Yet, my first thought is to put my things into boxes. The question, what am I leaving. And not where am I going. The sense of capitulating, estranging myself. A maladroit memorisation of the living.

...

Is it possible to walk too far?

...

If the question is not perambulatory then what is it?

...

What's it got?

...

I've lost my sense of this place. The sense of the directive. When for example I take several steps in the room, it is in the sense of which book. Why this book. Why for example Lanzmann or Duras rather than Giacometti. Why not. Why not something else. These are not questions. There are boxes which remain unopened and papers to put away. The thought of a thing.

...

Now the name Stéphane. It was inevitable. Stéphane from Nathanaël. One in the other, the two lovers wrapped in a single suffering body. Suffering for not being able to address one another other than in the echo that unmakes them.

...

I don't know about any of these forms, these lines—circle, spiral... Don't know which might apply. I think that it is always changing, perhaps something akin to Blanchot's line which forms a circle that doesn't close. But this is not necessarily a spiral, some segments disappear altogether, the way sand blows over a trail, the way a desert, in the night, redesigns itself, displacing its dunes, becoming unrecognisable. It is still recognisable as: desert, sand, but all of its trails are aporias (a path traced on water).

...

I could speak of this house for hours. The garden. I know it all. I know where the old doors are. All of it. The walls of the pond. All the plants. The location of all the plants. Even the wild plants. I know the place. All of it. (Duras)

...

At night I sleep with the door and the windows open. The door open onto the garden. The porch of which I say:

garden. If possible I would open the walls, the roof. The inside like the outside. And then the question, the one that has me asking how it is that I have so often chosen the wall instead of the window. The ground. When the door was right there, waiting for me.

...

It wasn't waiting.

...

At the theatre, it is from lack that everything is given to see. (Duras)

...

The problem is whether the cats really wish to be disturbed.— No.—I would like to sleep in my bed. I'd like to see the Atlantic Ocean.

...

There is no conflict. It is experienced alone. (Duras)

...

Not a single bed grants me sleep.

...

And if it were true that in going toward a place everyone were to die there. That upon arriving the world became unbearably small. And if this place were to welcome me. If it were the most unbearable thing of all. More unbearable than any other thing. For it to be reduced to the only place and for there to be nowhere else to go. And if I exhausted this entire possibility and desire all at once—

...

The house is a blank. I disappear inside.

...

Kiss the ocean for me.

...

Having never in my thinking connected *arrival* and *departure* as of two irreconcilable movements, I forgot the former term, the outlets lead nowhere. Departure alone comprised the whole movement, with neither beginning nor end, but an unconsidered end, and slow, sometimes coarse, and always furious, irreparable. For *arrival* would have meant: *Stay, die here.*

Chicago, Montréal
2008–2009, August

He dies like a horse, with an unsuspected force.

—*Marguerite Duras*

SUMMATION

It would then be necessary to be quiet, and for each to endeavor to go toward the violence of the other while dissipating his own.

—*Hervé Guibert*

Faced with the question, what does it matter what matters only to me ?

—*André Malraux*

Someone who, feeling himself abandoned, takes up a book, finds with a pang that the page he is about to turn is already cut, and that even here he is not needed.

—*Walter Benjamin*

Let someone rack his brains as to why I come walking along and stop him and shout at him, and let someone ask himself where I shall rush to, along what path I shall go with my thoughts when I rise again after this fall. What size shoes I take? How old I am? How I spend my money? When I was born? For a moment I had the idea of stating the size of my head, but it must be average. And my brain will weigh light after my death.

—*Ingeborg Bachmann*

Against it I don't know what I am staying.

...

If by liberation you intend the emancipation from reason, sure. If it's the thing that wracks groans and torment from the body, if at the moment of sleeping and waking it is the thing that transforms me into a howling cemetery, a blood-soaked battlefield. I have become the war and the sickness, the face of the death of a person. I have envisioned these technologies. (...) You see, if it isn't a liberation, it is nonetheless a thing detached against the thing that lays it bare. I am the residue of a self, the absence of relation: thing and thing.

...

Your name is discarded at the side of the road. After the months of deliberations. Thrown down among the gravel and algae of the pavement. This abandoned name is barely a death. It will happen to you one day in the mouth of another. That side-road name that holds the shape of your once-body. Your body in disbelief at not having that name.

...

With *him*, my *I-him*, in body, I have no further language. *He* grants me this reprieve.

...

My mind stops at the Bar Kokhba revolt and the collective suicide of the Guadeloupean maroons in 1802, alongside Mulâtresse Solitude. More than ever, I understand that decision. At the end of a battle, where nothing is ever won, the obvious and only possible act is to set fire to oneself. The enemy is nowhere visible, and the city, as it so often seems to be in my thinking, is empty, abandoned. What remains of it, I have ingested, in structure, in discourse, in enmity. The thing against which one fights becomes one. To obliterate it, surely it must be necessary to obliterate it in—and with—oneself. I cannot know what meaning to grant this in a present of abandon, of resentment, confusion and sorrow, of perverse euphoria. There are the cats who ask to be fed, and a love that surely doesn't intend for me, but toward which I go.

...

The absence of a witness is the beginning of a murder. It became clear to me at the crematorium when the howl, immediately swallowed by the roar of the furnaces, was torn from me.

...

Eyes open or closed, it's the same screen, the same blood, the same smell.

...

Desire's accusations are irrefutable. I come to you with judgement and morbidity. Against a theatre of moveable parts, Genet insists "the architecture of the theatre… must be fixed, immobilized, so that it can be recognized as responsible : it will be judged on its form." This, then, is my injunction, that I bring with me, my "irreversible" theatre. Judge me.

...

The conditional is bereaved: tense, unappeased. It carries potentiality's breach, boring into the undetermined with disbelief. The *if then* of me, constructed such that uncertainty, embedded in the causal palate of language's misdeed, is militantly rejected by a structuring of sated need. It locks into place, but this does nothing for a body that falls from a sky. The contaminant is alive, it is vital, distressed; it disregards our posturings. "Nothing is true," contends Édouard Glissant, "everything is alive." It is this untrue-alive, which is the end of I—its everlast. The insistence of Cahun's intransigent interrogation, speaking, alive: what want and to what end this accusation of endings? Each thing in ending, at the very start. It is sometimes called: onset. And we are its disease.

...

The bed expulses me. My head seized by a liquid burn.

...

We are in time. That, too, is unthinkable.

...

You arrive shortly after. Days, weeks. You say: N. You rid my names of their gravity, their fatality. N., a residue of me, a scrap. You open your mouth with mine, you gorge my cries, you pull my body under the weight of you, I bite into the soil of your shoulder, you cry the continent and the passing hour. You say nothing, you sleep and give me your rest, the livid days of tomorrows. You read to me out loud. You are my passeur, laid over my disappearance.

...

Who will wash the body of my death. Who will kiss my bloody mouth. Who will swallow my cries, my agony. Who will consume my passing. Who will speak (to) me.

...

I am bereft, and unjust. Now I can speak to you of this, now that I have written you I don't know what it will be with the telephone next time or the time after that, but it is okay now that I have told you and please be secretive with this, guard it like a wingless bird with no eyes, who never saw a thing and is afraid of loud noises. Make it precious that way and irrepressibly endangered, such that you have no desire to whisper it, not even to yourself.

...

Fistfully. Mouthfully. The place you take into you is an injury and my prints are all over you. This is your city. Your tawdry. As though speaking of seeing could correct calamity. Our limbs are not limber. And geography cringes at the encroachment of further geography. Find the text that granted permission, the book that wanted burning, the mouth that needed closing, the hand held before an expressionless face. Brazen and stumbling. (2006)

...

Death is long, terribly long, notwithstanding the unbearable remainder.

...

...and into your sleep, I swear it, into your death, I will follow you. (Koltès)

...

If it is true that "desire is dead, killed by an image," it may be that this accusatively emphatic image bespeaks the murderous vigil; to watch, unbidden. To bring the body, unworn, to testify against itself, to account for its enmity, build up the wall of its own figuration, severely, make what is seen visible against history's rent screen—a black box of miserly misery. Speak into speaking, unlistened. // I go to where it happens. The door is a door that closes. A gate that scrapes shut against a forensic, vaulted compound. These are its barbed technologies, its unmitigated heat, a fire that doesn't burn, a blood that doesn't bleed: the smell of it. If desire is dead it is dead at the point of seeing, accused, beseeching. It dies undead, it sees unspoken, it works its asphyxiation into the endangered throat, stripped of its vital civility, mouth open on no sound, untold. The wither image may have killed desire, ineradicably. Death's death as it were, remaindered at its skinned edge, its posthumous (re)iteration, end upon devastated end.

...

Through the window, the city demonstrates its refusal.

...

A. tells me that I am at the bottom of the pit. But it isn't at all that. A pit wouldn't be so bad. A bottom, an utterly agreeable thing. Even unbearably agreeable. But a bottom would be something. I wasn't able to tell her no, there is neither a bottom, nor a pit, nor a darkness, nor anything of the nihilistic dreams of the living. It's rather of the order of a blank. I think so. Vigilation is something like that. The attention granted to a thing to the point of the obliteration of looking and of the thing. That is where the voice is lost, touch evaporates, it burns for not being able to burn.

...

Saarbrücken: am in another language, as in a body of water that submerges me without touching a thing.

...

One must agree to be finished: to be here and nowhere else, to do this and no other thing, now and not never nor ever ...to have this life alone. (André Gorz)

...

An overly aggrieved body, a face that carries several deaths already, including mine, and the murder of the mother, the brother. Who will ever want this mouth?

...

Crossing the square, I feel an utter disgust toward all these humans, I tell myself that it's everywhere the same people, that it's no surprise we perpetuate the same violences, just look at us. It isn't that we don't love enough, I think perhaps it is that we don't hate one another enough. The human being is a botched animal.

...

You dance because you are aware of death. (Pippo Delbono)

...

I continue to scatter myself to the wind, I'm in shreds in these places that seem to come to pieces as I move through them, as though my presence alone conferred their disintegration.

...

Wien: An unthinkable world.

...

November (end). Today I would like to speak to you. I know that you would have something to say to me, to me and to all of this, and that you would take me somewhere on foot, that you would have a thing or two to show me. I can't imagine going back, but remaining is just as improbable. As for me, I would like one day to kiss your mouth and wonder whether mine is even capable of such a thing. Love from a loveless city. N.

...

My words tonight before a Viennese public in an old hospital reconstituted as a *Universität* made my mouth into a crypt and purged the last vital energies from the room. Ending unspeaking unbreathing and the room unsound. It is a disconcerting shame that accompanies a death, for the person remaining, the vitally-residual, with her culpable vitality, a fistful of aschenglorie, a scattered self. And a face which must only signify this from now on.

...

Kafka: My love for you doesn't love itself. (Gorz)

...

The body is seized, inert, beating, palpitating, an anguish in time. Is it me.

...

Deutschland: I go toward everything as though I were late, our late desires, yes. It isn't a place I would have chosen for myself. But one doesn't choose one's self.

...

The narrative of the end of a certain time is told in a new time which retains that end—an end by which it presents itself as beginning. (Lyotard)

...

Between two places, in a despotic airport (Frankfurt), I write my hope for an inevitable *outre mesure*. Might it be, in the end, a matter of "that unforgottenness of forgetting that isn't memory"? (Malraux).

...

Unmoorings.

...

From part to parting, to be summoned is to be attentive

to the tide that founds and founders being, I mean the eventuality of one's *existere*, of one's situation.

...

Vienna is not a city.

...

RY King's photographic dissolve marks the paper immutable. Immutable in that it is always imbricated in a mechanism of deterioration. In this improper sense, the image is not separable from its degradation. Its substances are both paper and light. Thus they are neither, as they run into each other. The bird, in this instance, which is scarcely discernible, is in a field of apparent surfaces. It comprises the surface by which it becomes visible, an irregularity on a structure of hay-bales in a field of depleted colour. The photograph misdirects its intention. It intends for me to fall in. In to America.

...

It comes with a number, assigned to a calcined human body which is incommunicable: . When it says "…I need catastrophes, coups de théâtre," it abandons sense. The lake is up to my knees in November.

...

The time of the photograph is (always) after. This imprecision accommodates the numerous successions, the end upon seismic end. In a time without time, un(re)countable: still. In this, it is a perfect crime, "the annihilation annihilated, the end...deprived of itself."

...

Are you the sum of your cities? What are your cities? "Wounded mouths that gape onto the void"? (Lyotard)

...

I crossed over, I touched, I howled, I gave, I envisioned, I was afraid and I went toward everything that seemed to go against me. I said yes in spite of myself, while saying never again—not Germany, not Austria, not America, not anywhere ever, especially not me—and it's this conjunction surely that means that I exist in the rapacious non-existence of the delirious (mis)deed.

...

Pain and pain again. But it isn't mine, in that it does not belong.

...

This trip to Germany and Austria was by turns very exacting, and always very emotional; I learned a lot, about myself, about history, about the very violence of my hopes. Vienna especially plied me, with its architecture of pomp and excess, I hardly slept. Presents and pasts combined and I was suffocating…I was suffocating and this didn't prevent me from feeling just as intensely the warmth with which I was everywhere welcomed. I emerge from it shaken, my head shattered, my body plunged into that (for me) beginning conversation and I am moved by the openings—gentle and violent—that sought me out. There is no turning away from it. I go to that which exceeds comprehension, the furore of history, the aleatory encounters, the receptiveness of a present within voice's reach.

...

Time carries on, how curious, one doesn't imagine that it could at such an hour.

...

"for we say here: the time before the fire and time after it." (in Şenocak)

...

Life's chance is death's behest.

...

... a stable, several rooms, bicycle rides in the countryside, a terrible parking lot, people coming and going, a threat, unnamed, an art show perhaps, and the rapid deterioration of my body in the face of everyone. Lying down or standing, the liquefaction of my joints, my bones floating in my remains, gaping holes at my knees, waxen skin, saying to R. who is watching television with several others, kill me, have mercy, why won't you kill me. A boy underneath a blanket, but nothing was fixed, it must have been the residual death imprinted in the body, my installation in that savagery, its imprint of undesirability, tear me from this sleep.

...

As for this end, attached to a death, I am the one now who is changed by it, and who rejects certain narratives which make me into something I don't want to be.

...

I make the connection between these texts and the sprig of creosote in the mail, your wanderments and a detailed attention granted to the unsuspected details of a fragile narrative of seasons and their material. The documentation of this—burst and furling. A magisterial museum, the one that isn't edified. I admire your eye and what empties from it, the residue of a gaze is a form of (formless) archive.

...

We could think of the sense of touch as the unconscious of vision. (Pallasmaa)

...

It's 3:30 p.m., time for me to sleep. I've already had one nap, twice gone around the neighbourhood, made and unmade the bed, adored the cats, prepared inedible foods, drunk the remaining tea, written several letters, taken some notes and checked the mail that doesn't come. It's impossible to make these tasks into a day, the day being obstinately out of reach, the door being unrecognisable, one walks into it, face first, still there is some relief in the sensation.

...

The next text is a kind of suppuration. It must be the equivalent of rubbing gravel and glass into a wound, but I must do this violence to myself now. Press my whole face into the ambient abjection, hatred, rage. Perhaps remove a blistered skin, rendering myself raw and possibly more humane.

...

The cities of Saarbrücken, Wien and Freiburg made a strong impression on me and I come away from them removed from an important conversation. The technologies of transportation being what they are, we are propelled too quickly over the surface of the earth, and I find myself scattered in all those cities and others as well. As a result, I walk in these streets of Chicago with bits of Freiburg or Vienna still stuck to me as well as the echo of a language I barely had time to encounter or to begin to signify.

...

It's true, I am a hermaphrodite and you must be an angel. De Beauvoir says that hermaphrodites are of neither sex and angels, both. How is it that a philosopher can have a serious discussion about angels? I don't mind. I think you can be an angel and maintain integrity. My hermaphroditism makes me very vulnerable, but you have wings, you can fly. Now that we are back in the realm of paper airplanes, I should probably climb into bed before I mistake the window for a door and go swimming in concrete. You see, I am dreaming already.

...

The angel of death is the one who comes after.

...

All this language in my mouth, S., is the matter of death. I haven't the courage, the obstinacy, the capacity, to speak against speaking, to speak against my own silences, to open what is so visibly destructive. It destroys me and I agree to this destruction. I undo a pile of books on a shelf: a note addressed to me by J., books brought back from my last trips to Toronto and Montréal (six months ago already), a postcard from Germany, and in my desk drawer twenty-three paper sheaths for chopsticks. The paintings sequester me. I try to move them and can't. Even B.'s drawing is becoming unbearable. And underneath, my absolute stupidity, my impropriety, I want to get rid of everything, but am caught in this body with these insignificant pains, and utterly incapacitated. Breathe. I breathe. But what air is this? If not the air of all the bombed cities. We are not done burying ourselves.

...

R.: The city was very much dead as it should have been and I was ashamed to be there.

...

Before opening it, I am curious about this envelope patched with tape that contains the purple ink of a stained finger.

What hesitation sealed then tore then sealed it again?

...

To be able even clumsily to approach this form
(photography) which you embody—its materiality, which
alone is a seduction and a much more impressive enigma
than any language will ever be.

...

Together, with our mouths, we will learn again. We may be
improbable, but we are not impossible.

...

If the text here is meant to attest to something, to give
presence to a conversation that had its moment of
becoming, it risks, I think, paralysis, or stagnation, in the
form we are trying to grant it, its rigidification in writing,
in writing out what came first from a mouth, which in this
sense makes a transcribed conversation into something
that is not-writing, that may be unaccountable—but to
what—or perhaps unaccounted for, and I hope now that
it may be possible to find a way to account for what went
missing, what disappeared into "that damp yellow smoke
thrown from the chimney / losing itself in the downcast
sky" (*Sudden Orpheus*). The dead die their deaths and we

may be present with them, and it is not hyperbole I think, to say that this death, the apprehension of that morbidity, is in our languages, and the fixing here, of a text, is some part interment, some part remainder, and what is to be done with this ash, if not to throw it to the wind. But it comes back at us as surely as we run from it.

...

Who, though I screamed, would hear me amongst the ranks / of the angels? (Rilke)

...

The angel of death is not a carrier of death unless he is the one who carries death into the after of survivors, but he doesn't carry death, for death is always already awaiting him, that angel of death in the present of excessions.

...

I turn toward German to calm my fear of German. *Denn Bleiben ist nirgends.* (Rilke)

...

There is a passage, toward the end of the book, which

interrogates the question of memory, of memorialisation, in the very quick of its intimacy: "The paradox here is that if the only one bearing witness to the human is the one whose humanity has been wholly destroyed, this means that the identity between human and inhuman is never perfect and that it is not truly possible to destroy the human, that something always *remains. The witness is this remnant.*" I follow Agamben when he qualifies the witness with remains, but I am not persuaded that this is an indication of a human quality. Unless the human is abject, partial, cleaved, a breach in the place of that which is broken, destroyed. What remains, I think, the incessance of the horror, which finds a reiterative form in the place in which it might situate itself, and that may be where the question of an ethics might be located, might be about to be approached.

...

The days once more unbearable. Sunday's visit to the studio, thinking about the *mahnmal*, the outside, and when I wake early in the morning, sometimes before four, my jaw is so tight that I fear all the bones in my head will shatter.

...

A pain that hollows as I read you, in the place of our friendship. It is not enough to wash the body of a death, nor to see it burn.

...

The muscle that follows is a muscle of grief. (Rachel Gontijo Araújo)

...

Your death prepares mine. I say this to you. I say that you have just arrived a little bit early. I say it but there is no one to say it to. You, for example.

...

Which makes of you: not anyone anymore.

...

You must have noticed that I am a reader of great impatience, and sufficiently misanthropic at times. Admittedly, I recognise this to be in contradiction with my desire for dialogue, with you for example, in these letters which deploy the spaces surrounding us and having undoubtedly anticipated our encounter in that terrible auditorium of the Universität where not only Heidegger, but Benjamin, must have sat. I have such a strong desire to speak to you, to meet you.

...

, I am convoked by the exactitude of your suggestion that *one listens with one's voice*. The paradox, then, of the breach, might be that in the act of speaking-listening, one throat becomes unbound from another (Lyotard-Malraux), and this is experienced as a betrayal, or a defection. This violence lays perhaps in wait at the bottom of speaking or listening, it may already be in place and dialogue may simply exist along its fragile and catastrophic edge, anticipating the necessary disaster of unboundedness. To be torn (one) from the other. Mind you nothing prepares one for the end of the voice, torn from the space surrounding a body irrevocably amputated of its meaning, of death itself, and I know it for having seen it with my mouth that the last sound is pulled into and not out of the body, there is no saying: *expiration*.

...

"What will be done to us, *after?*" (René Char)

...

And forgetting—*Vergessen?*—is something I have calculated into my life, precisely as a means of (dis)figuring language.

...

NN, a double name, a name stripped of name, in which to disappear, *Nomen Nescio*, out of which one might not exist, an I, for example, exemplar of nothing, a name that might also be stripped of place, of origin, of engendering, because naming is a violence that, evidently, cannot not be undone.

...

The reasoned conclusion to the slow holocausting of a person by modern medicine with its "treatments" derived from chemical warfare, and its military diction. Why should I speak any more of this than already I have done? This conversation with its specific humiliations and barbarity does not interest me, and it is not a conversation anymore. It is simply a lost thing and the litany is exacerbating.

...

In the time of the death of the painter, I wrote books and a pigeon died in the street. I crossed an ocean. I touched several cities. I said.

...

The letter commits an ill that exists in time. "Please, believe again this notion of my voice; remember / what it is to touch me. I ask because this isn't speaking; this is a kind of walking to the river." (Brian Teare) I have not, like you, the vastness of the ocean to behold.

...

Have I not the same responsibility to the century as to the instant?

...

Yes, the "I" must be re-imagined. The pronoun indicating the first person, the human subject has to be one of the most crucial and most cruel parts of speech. Bearing such strong lines and given so much weight. It configures us; it destroys us. And we say parts of speech? What part of speech am I if I have no speech? What if interests that are never mine mutilate my "I"? (Christine Stewart)

...

At the end of *The Trial* there is—"Like a dog. As though the shame of it would outlast him."—Might I have become that "shame"?

...

We have a great responsibility toward the animals we have decided to domesticate. It's obvious that our bad habits are destructive, as they are beginning to develop human illnesses, some of which are congenital, because of breeding practices. Often I think that we humans give only the worst of ourselves.

...

, and I thought that an entire city like that, its areas, can also mourn a single person, alone in his death, alone and trembling. It is perhaps also a form of love, to love in absence, the person one has loved, most awkwardly, during these years. In the studio, I found self-portraits. Marvellous. Astonishing.

...

I have so much to say on this subject that I prefer to say nothing. I fear otherwise that in opening myself I will never close again. The wound, I believe it, must remain gaping. In this sense, if philosophy intensifies the question such as it is asked, I do want to believe that in philosophy we are with the question of death. If, however, it seeks an answer where there is none, it is of no interest to me. The greatest indecency, it seems to me, is to attempt to close the question of death. But to answer to it—to take my responsibility before this death—that is something else. Sometimes I think that I have lived all my life in the sense of these instants. At present, they summon me irrevocably. Fear is a thing lesser than fear. A thing that exceeds it also. There is nothing.

...

In such little time, I witnessed the attempts of a person who wanted to grant meaning to loss. But it cannot be reasoned. Unless reasoning rips the stitch that frantically attempts to cohere that which is forcibly incoherent. A language. That, too, can be a death.

...

I want to be able to say that I was standing on that road and that I lay against the same animals, but it isn't true. It was another road, and my body leaned against other bodies, their seizure, their exhaustion. I was covered in blood and it wasn't enough. And the howling that came later stayed caught in my skin.

...

Sprachlos. // Bitte.

...

And there, set upon a box near the plants that I water in *your stead*, I fall upon the dictionary, as though by your hand you had tendered it to me.

...

He doesn't know that I leave the apartment at 8:36 p.m. and that I take the train with your photograph in my jacket pocket with the express intent of showing it to him. That our encounter lasts no more than two or three minutes and is of no consequence. He looks at the photograph and identifies you in his memory. Gravely, he says yes, he says it a second time as though to reassure himself of something, he confirms to me that you existed once, in this bookstore where you would go and where he has been working for nine and a half years, he tells me. This time, I do not cry, simply I say thank you and I walk out.

...

Otherwise people won't understand what magnificent sense it made that they pierced his night-shirt and stabbed him all over his body, to see if they would strike the hard core of a personality. (Rilke)

...

Without you the year comes to an end. A face ripped off, a hand that strikes nothing.

...

I break my arms so as not to have to hold anymore.

...

...periods of happiness are empty pages in history, for they are the periods of harmony, times when the antithesis is missing. (Hegel) If it weren't for these words of Hegel's, I'd split my face open on the porcelain. Might that be the antithesis?

...

It seems to me something of a consumerist tendency, the way in which new (academic, artistic) theories are produced, consumed, abandoned, crossed out in several months, if that. The missing matter is time. This more than anything painting is teaching me. The time of things – of a canvas, for example, in a field of light, over a period of several days, only begins to be seen. It is discreet, almost prudish, easy to overlook if one refuses to take time with it. And of course, sadistically, time takes all of its time, and ours, what do you think?

...

This book belongs to another time. It no longer knows that I existed.

...

B. writes me from Berlin to announce that he caught a glimpse of me in the body of a boy in a café of the Gendarmemarkt. A lapsus has me substitute the other word with *Gendermarkt*.

...

Yesterday I was able to read the first line of a poem by Rilke without the help of a dictionary. *Ich lebe mein Leben in Wachsenden Ringen*, but I want quickly to return to Celan. Celan must be read slowly. His work is friable and sharp and breaks the bones of the reading body so imperceptibly that one hardly realises it until one finds oneself slumped in one's seat and incapable of rising again.

...

Bureacracy kills death. So I am thickening the walls around me as my skin thins. And I lean closer to the ground where I am less easily identifiable.

...

K. tells me that grief is an open-heart surgery. The organs are all exposed and people stick their fingers in it. But I prefer the word *sorrow*. It doesn't presuppose an end.

...

Back then. Always back then, about which he knew nothing. (Bachmann)

...

I would like to send you a book. It's a terribly ugly object, but a text of some importance to me, and which is relevant to our conversations in Saarbrücken. A destructive book as well, and which precedes...*s'arrête? Je* which you know to be unreadable. As though in writing it I had stopped French short, killed the killing word. Since then, I have been writing these notebooks which are attempts at writing, essays, small failures that try impossibly to put together time and its sense.

...

Is it true that we are living these years? This way we have of counting, one step and then the next, while it really is only a slow slide without even the assurance of some nothingness. Is this a letter for a new year? Hardly. But then, is this a body for a time?

...

I told myself that I ought to have inserted each blade into my skin in order to retain something of its memory, the scalding extraction. At present I am nothing but flame and frozen brow. I don't wish to be consoled. I want only for the bruise to be visible.

...

What would happen if you let the horses run away with you?

...

We are inhabited by banal monsters. // No religion, no experience teaches us that the horror is *in us*. (...) The monster occupied my remains, then my conscience which was losing itself in sleep; finally, that road dissipated—but I had recognised it, I will recognise it, like those dreams in which we think; I've dreamed that before. (Malraux)

...

The march before survival.

...

As for tomorrow, I would like (*Ich möchte*) to be able to push Heidegger's university down the hill. All universities probably deserve to be thrown overboard or pushed down all the hills of the world. The result might actually be *interesting*, though no doubt *unbegreiflich*, and it's just as well.

...

But where does the end of life begin? Not when, but *where*? (Pierre Fédida)

...

Le Diamant: On such a day as this, I would want to have the necessary courage to kill myself. To take the path at the foot of Morne Larcher and take my plunge. But there is a desire that exceeds this one. A desire…to exist, no doubt; even this pain is something. And anyway, how is one to kill something that isn't quite alive?

...

These are simply the thoughts of a person disastered by sleep and whose mouth is stuffed full of death.

...

Various infrastructures and terrains, materials and registers.

A raised voice, a sandy hill, a water bottle, my father. An irascible doctor, a dying man, a phone call, a set of stairs. Several distances. An inventory. Running. A conversation with a loved one.

...

The dream came apart as I was projecting myself into the darkness of the room, leaving the bed to open the sliding door onto the balcony, leaving me with these few impressions, and the sense of having lost something, at the very moment at which I was trying to reverse time in order to take from it something that was already escaping me.

...

There is no return. There was never a way there. (Bachmann)

...

Sub-tending beauty there is this as well, which is unlimited and trembling. One land beneath another land that is bridled. (Haïti, for example, with its earthquake and the numerous aftershocks. But that too is history: a calamity).

...

Thus do I draw up a part of my past, for the times before when I was very young and incapable of that refusal. But you see, I would have had to have extracted my own corpse from the mud of another time in order to accomplish this, in order to give a voice to a part of me that is dead, assassinated, that I no doubt killed myself before someone else could, or precisely because someone else did, precisely so as not to have to listen to such things. In order not to exist.

...

My relationship to places is often subterranean (to avoid saying *subconscious*, also because the relationship is *telluric*—abstract, no doubt, but not ethereal). Thus, as with my trip to Wien and Freiburg, this trip to Martinique provoked internal disturbances. Still, it managed to dislodge something, and so I return to Chicago somewhat less encumbered.

...

I think of going out, of entering this dark city and walking until it is expulsed from my body, until the roads turn to fields and the lamp-posts give way to stars, until place has exhausted itself and there is nothing left but the limits of other places, other languages, other forms of interpolation. And were it possible, I would abandon myself there.

...

What is a life capable of when the forces that grant it desire are as powerful as the forces of resistance?

...

I would like to be elsewhere. In this place, too great a pressure is exerted and too great a solitude. If it is a matter of being alone, better to be on board a train crossing another country, in a hotel on a sea, in some marsh, like Gide's Tityre.

...

In fact it is exactly a matter of thresholds. The body as threshold, and there, the door. For you, the term is *animal*, for me, littoral. Each and each are at the very limits of language, where our senses are confounded.

...

Unlike Ionesco, it isn't the night that fills me with horror, but the middle of the day.

...

My practice assumes the wreckage of history, both artistic and cultural, and is in no sense "pure." (Jeff Marlin)

...

This day is so close to all the other days.

...

Germany and its seductions. What an improbable sentence...

...

Today, I would like for these walls to be more thick or the room more elevated, or else level with the earth. // I think of setting fire to the fragile marshes, to the herons and cormorants. I think of Collobert's suicide, an animal that suffers, trains that go very fast. A small boat in the middle of a lake. A sky that produces water and an earth that does the same. // And I wonder: what must we retain?

...

What can you do? In German, *I would like* is pronounced *Ich möchte* and the sentences remain there, gaping, like an incomplete word. The world (*Welt*) closed against a mouth (*Mund*).

...

Tomorrow in a room I will open my mouth and words will come out. Friday, I'll attend a talk on Paul Celan. This is how I mark the days. This is how I introduce movement into my body, as a reminder of a vital and forgotten thing, beyond the anesthetized immediate.

...

The sea was going to devour me. Incessant. My room just there, several metres from the precipice, the edge. My foot along that single strand. I walked it. // At present it is cold again and I am living in this city.

...

An einem Abend der fassungslosen Traurigkeit... (Adorno)

...

At present I am writing to you in time, through and against time, because you are not there to receive these words. But they will wait for you, a sort of *poste restante*, on your return.

...

Who are you? I am a person who walks in the mouth of the world.

...

Unique en son genre. Perhaps, but not for long. Soon I will be in a state of decomposition just like everyone.

...

Even the smell of ash dissipates.

...

I was dizzy, a vertiginous precipice, an eventual emotion, to which I cannot risk attributing a language. It's possible that the nomination of every thing at present signals the promise of a destruction. The incitement to an end.

...

The hammer blows come after; they strike my head, my bones, they make echoes out of sounds I don't recognise, and my breath catches, it hooks into a chipped part of me that hooks into a chipped part of the world.

...

To it alone, I would not exist.

...

Now I say, no, this is just what I want, if it is impossible, it is impossible; I will try it, though I do not know how it should be done. (Van Gogh)

...

The nakedness of ages renders me fragile, plies the spine of centuries, pervades me with stone and splits the cold. That's when I light the fire and open the doors.

...

your mouth his one sure dream / of sleep. (Teare)

...

It isn't clear whether it is the absence of a *name* or whether it is you who see seeing the scoring of this letter that renders it unwritable.

...

Taking these words into one's mouth. Being responsible for them. We touched them after all. // (After all that we continue to touch). // This problem is resolvable neither in situation nor in syntax. But I am not seeking a resolution. Just the formulation of a question, and it keeps changing sense.

...

The thing: is it found or given or taken that which is already taken away?

...

For example, I learn that the German for word is *Mund*, which calls up the French *monde* (world, in German, *Welt*, returns to English in the form of a sore). This is no reliable etymology, but the synaptic folds register these aberrations. The body marked mute speaks beyond itself in the mouths of others, doesn't it? At the beginning there are the mouths of others on our skin. We don't ask for this. After when we do ask, can we be sure to know where the question comes from?

...

That the book without me.

...

I am not afraid. Disappointed, that's all.

...

Regardless of what is written, what is said, the city continues as it will, and we become the willing executioners of the world.

...

I stopped saying it. First I could not say it, then I stopped saying it.

...

When one is cut from the world, one has recourse to the part of the self that flees the world; in other words the part which exonerates itself of its share of responsibility, the one that closes the mouth over the incomplete re-speak.

...

On board the train toward O'Hare, while reading Brian Teare's *Rooms*, I fall upon something so embarrassingly obvious—embarrassing because it is obvious—which reads me (and rids me) in keeping with apartment 1020 in which we changed places in 1983. The transposition of the schema of internal displacements and voyages signals a fatality that I would like to be able to disavow. For having been expulsed from my room to surrender my place to the repatriated son, and finding myself next to my sister in her bed for the duration of the infanticide, I caught an internal exile from the time of the son's occupation of that childhood. Thus were the subsequent departures provoked, at least in part, by the displacement along several metres down a hallway in a more or less fateful May or June. Which leads me to find myself in Montréal (the *unoccupied* place of my birth, a place therefore of flight and violences which had preceded me, but irrefutably marked by the *absence* of a domicile), the apprehended and sought-after exile. The impossibility of *dwelling* then offers itself as evidence. Wherever I am, I am already anticipating the *coup de grâce* that will put an end to me in my bed beneath the body of a familiar-stranger and dismiss me therefrom. *There* where I bind my bedridden flight to my sister inscribing in her sleep my fugitive complaint.

...

Franz Schürch: All strangled because the fire deserves you.

...

Without warning I leave Montréal to return to Chicago. On a wide country gravel road, I walk past the construction site of a house where three men are jostling one another on a railing, one knocking another over onto the ground.

There are people about. A demonstration? It seems more like an exodus, a departure precipitated by what? The group is now on this road, now in an institutional hall of sorts (university or shopping mall?). A woman calls out to me; she wants me. I only see her from behind. Run! I want to run from her (familiarity?). In the apartment — Chicago or Montréal or elsewhere?—a strange woman pulls me toward her in my bed and rejects me instantly. She cries out in accusation, I put my clothes back on. I go to turn on the lights but the switches don't work. This isn't my apartment, it is where I am. The sense that I am lodged in a dormitory or a hotel room that eventually turns into an airport. I call the concierge urgently, he comes up and turns on the lights without difficulty. When we are in the bathroom, I open the shower, I am naked. He closes the curtain behind me. The cat (there is one cat, no, there are two), escapes through the door left open by the concierge. He runs into the neighbour's apartment (a group of young people). I run after him, wrapped in a towel and manage to get him to turn back. At an advanced hour of the day I still haven't booked a return ticket to Montréal where I am expected to be at an event that very evening. It isn't only the prospect of missing this engagement that worries me, but the fact also of having missed my departure, for the other half of the ticket remains unused.

...

Destruction awaits anyone who, answering to his vocation and fulfilling it, exerts himself within history; (Cioran)

...

One would have only to speak of oneself in the past tense, in order to become accustomed to one's (over)coming disappearance.

...

One always perishes by the self one assumes: to bear a name is to claim an exact mode of collapse. (Cioran) Thus is every name a kind of suicide that tears the name from the self in order to enable the existence of other selves, of another (than the) self. The simultaneities are disjunctive and inscribe breaches that annul the self at the very moment at which it is provisionally embodied. Every suicide runs the risk of being botched as well as that of succeeding.

...

It is by breaking that one is made, makes oneself.

...

Den wir, wo wir fühlen, verflüchtigen; ach wir // atmen uns aus und dahin; (Rilke)

...

One of the conditions of existing is to not exist.

...

I open a notebook onto several letters begun over the past few months. What movement of discomfort prevented me from sending them? This writing in a void is a writing of avoidance, of an unaccomplished act, of touch, stricken. Tell me, without reading me, swallow the sound into the unspoken mouth, implore the city beneath my feet to subsist me against a fateful non-existence. Isn't.

...

Occurs in absolute retreat, the resistance and hazard of a supplement of emotion. It's just the door I am passing, that you tender to me without yourself knowing how to pass it. This is as it happens, beneath a frozen rain, in a lorry as I am driving. Everything else indicates otherwise. It's April, you defend yourself poorly in time and in circumstance. Nonetheless I open and note what is happening, the none being annunciatory of the never that is arrived at.

...

I forget: the Mexican tile, two books, the tea-bag, a favourite dessert.

...

Malraux's "je-sans-moi" speaks to the non-existence that he accounts for. But it is the avowal—in language—of the improbability of his vitality. To live, then, would be to wager on that near-nothing, and speaking projects it into the after of an echo without succession.

...

I miss, but it is misattributed.

...

The first time I listened to the Villa-Lobos I am sending you, I was driving in the country. A long time ago now, 1998 or 1999. I stopped the car to listen. I was overwhelmed. I listened and I cried and I was on my way. This morning as I read you, that voice comes back to me. A voice that seems to come out of nowhere—*Nirgendwo*—and by its unsituatedness, makes its vibration into a place.

...

The voice, a drain.

...

In Cioran, I find this: "Every work turns against its author. The poem will crush the poet, the system the philosopher, the event the man of action." But this crushing, it seems, is the primary material of a life of so-called engagement— the crushing requires a response. Is it as much a matter of intention as of intent? Derrida insists: "You, it has to be you." It's the *incipit*—

...

It's almost *Paper City* all over again, except that *n* and *b* have fallen from their skies.

...

This word *specimen* obliterates me.

...

The task I have given myself is equivalent to stripping an immense cemetery covered in bones. I must move with lightness and deference, taking care not to inter myself inadvertently.

...

The rippling horse you extend, I go toward it.

...

The sense, sometimes, that I am reliving you.

...

Texts that form an object at last. We believe them to be tangible. A work endures. The writer is not an artist because of this. Matter is not his responsibility. He pursues it. It's laughable. He has to make do. Writing was not invented by a writer. (Christophe Donner)

...

Montréal arrives at me.

...

You didn't dare say: *come*. Me, in your place, I would have said: *do nothing but come*. But I didn't dare.

...

Why must love take on the aspect of a fault? I trust you achingly. And I think that you don't blame me too much.

...

I write letters which I no longer send.

...

Massive collapse; desire to split my head open on a swift and crude surface. I cry and that's all. It's far worse.

...

You constituted yourself as a museum. In life you guarded against death by burying in the inconceivable soil of existence everything that by anticipation you agreed to inhume. The very matter of what you called life was a matter of enclosure, your body as well, which you rejected. You would have made me into the crypt of a consumption I had already become unaccustomed to. The museum of you, into which you have made me the heir is a clumsy shield against my stricken temperament. I blow the walls apart. I straddle the railings. I go to the excess-of-you in order to be able to leave the disavowed place. I don't fall to pieces, I walk on the shards, bleed and displace myself, say, come. And I come. Moulted. Torpid.

...

A-more as isolate I, reverberant in and past the breath that sustains—that withstands—it. Vital, this force, and so mortal. When it ends what end does it achieve as it carries on past its own, self-seeking. More's excess is the self's burden. It is grasped at and unreached, brimming. To say I is to acknowledge what is borne. An ethics of foremost and fathom. It carries that violence also, of extraction, separating sound from voice, before even coming to speaking. This I might be the voice of its own extradition, formulating the expulsions that are a condition of engaged existence: speaking past the self into what is both anticipated and forgotten. An I to remember oneself by, in the advent of one's meaning, intention to mean.

...

I don't eat. I am hungry and I don't eat. It isn't asceticism. Sometimes I don't eat out of disgust, sometimes out of excessive hunger. The very sight of food disgusts me. Not so much the food itself but myself before it. What more can you possibly want? I am so stuffed full of world that I can't take another thing into me. Desire that kills desire. Abjection.

...

Chicago and I: we evacuate one another mutually.

...

I wanted to become disinterested in everything. To cease.

...

Saturday is suicidal. Sunday is superfluous.

...

I don't know whether I must write or be silent, drive myself into concrete.

...

I can want a city that stands cold in itself and then warms in spring. I can want a city to want me even if a city doesn't know what want tastes like. Even if I can't say to the city: Put your hand here. (Suzanne Hancock)

...

To give one's word to desire is to speak the perdition of desiring. In the perdition that is this desire, there is endurance. The endurance of the given word.

...

Je vais m'envahir is three times leaving. The going of *je vais,* the leaving of *m'enva* and the Spanish *ir*. Must this sentence be read as three attempted suicides, three attempted escapes? Whatever it is, the declaration is defeated.

...

For if this desire doesn't exist, what then can exist? (Stig Dagerman)

...

I bring myself closer to suicide and tell myself that this is still a way to live.

...

Being born or dying: *I* arrives at you.

...

I have the dream in which you take me by the hand.

...

You mortal, more me. Thr'

...

I want to say *self*, the (un)(m)asked je, in ambiguity, but it is in the mouth, I hear it, the mouth, in speaking, jeers.

...

No matter. I try not to think like this. Montréal at last. Body at an end. Cryptic city. No, I can't, it's spring after all and there are the cats, your two postcards on my desk in Chicago and the light on Chabot. "When I think of what I've experienced, it seems that all I did was lose my bodies along the way." (Clarice Lispector)

...

I set about German the way one sets about eating a meal at a table. I decide to eat that particular death. Celan via Blanchot, Bachmann by Jaccottet. Turn the wound in French, immobilise myself on the Franco-German front where I suffer more than one defeat. Because there is no certainty that the Nietzsche I am reading via Kaufmann in French is the same one that Derrida, etc. I regurgitate and it's just as well. Because *heute*, today, isn't the same *heute* as today. Isn't the same suicide.

...

It's Friday I am preparing your death. Your death which arrives at me. I choke on the stones of this city where you are not. The man in the street says this word, nothing, he sings it. I walk inside the vibration of this word that doesn't belong to me anymore than any other word, pronounced differently. Friday, J. is beaten in the stairs. Saturday you howl through the night. Sunday I go to the market. After, it's Monday. After. October, March.

...

And yet, always we choose a companion for ourselves: not for ourselves but for something inside us, outside of us, that needs us to be lacking for ourselves in order to pass the line we will not reach. (Blanchot)

...

Tonight the hours passed. With or without me. It's the same work of extraction. No echo resonates. I light no candles. I don't listen to Shostakovich. There is the silence D. qualified as unbearable. This place smothers noise. I rise and I sleep silenced. It isn't clear that it is verifiable, existence, mine I mean. A sorrow that is too heavy and too light. Have so often been mistaken.

...

Hermaphrodite is a word desired by an unintelligible body.

...

I say that the attack, the breach, is desirable, that regardless we are not whole, never whole. Guibert, *the cancerous image*, the offence of looking, of taking, touch, the stain.

...

Strain.

...

It isn't you, it's the idea I have of you.

...

We are unforeseen and uncalled for. Hermaphroditism might be just that, a plunge into the desiring body far from nominal preoccupations. Masculine and feminine or rather neither, in other words elsewhere, which for me is an act of presence: *there*. Away from decided forms of determined political discourse, but instead: *facing one another*. This too is unintelligible. To be caught off guard is nonetheless to give oneself to the instant. The instant in its duration.

...

Why must my heart beat there?

...

(an author without a text writing nonetheless, a spectre— *sombra*—of herself, the spectre of her spectre and imminent with it.)

...

I mourn the places and the passing ours.

...

In the end I cried over all of my cities. Leaving, as one leaves a lover one has not stopped loving.

...

The city is sheared in layers, the whole of it suddenly exposed. I think that death must be like that, the confrontation of every temporality, a life, and more than a life, the cities all superimposed, offering to each a wrenching, desperate and hatefully exquisite grasp. The enchanting offering of a void—the having been.

...

I who was born exterminable, that's why I'm alive. (Roland Castro)

...

The man in the street calls out to me. He wants to know my origins. He tells me his and those of the photographs he would like to sell, he invents a complicity between us. I listen, I say nothing, I have no need for complicity or origin and his dream such as he relates it to me is a tiresome dream. I almost don't notice the moon in the sky. And your name, he insists, extending a hand I shake despite myself. Nathanaël, I say, as I turn to leave. Perplexed, he wants me to clarify: *e-l-l-e?* No, I answer, and I go.

...

The realisation that I was not alone in the world was unbearable. That J. could have taken the same bridge as I in Wien. That P.'s eyes also rested there, in a country that ought to belong to no one. That É. could anticipate my arrival in that place ruined for me every possible elsewhere. It wasn't for the sake of purity, far from it, but the assurance, that I knew to be false and accidental, that I might exist in places I had not yet been, where my existence remained yet unverifiable, in other words imminent. I wanted for no one to tell me what was, for no one to come and correct the error of my approach through the intermediary of historical or political corrections, for the place to be thus rendered banal, not to be, so to speak, and by anticipation, thus obliterated. I wanted language unspoken; the approach unbegun; the walk along this particular wall inexperienced. Not mine, and not mined either.

...

And it was necessary for me to unfasten myself from these things, though each gesture seemed a crime to me, the murder of a self, and of the painter as well. The consolidation of a death. Love from this end of Chicago.

...

Soon our letters will be marked elsewhere.

...

The days remove me. I think sometimes that I am not careful enough with my sorrow. That I have betrayed something essential—of him in me.

...

Saturday, I hand over the studio.

...

I turn out.

...

How far must the hollow hollow? I roll myself up, I sleep with my head under the covers I draw my knees to my chin and I hate myself for being alive. And these words in my books hammer the inside of my head and I hate myself also for having written them. And I think—I know—that the course of the letter sent from the desert to the city is the trace of our friendship which is also a love, and I hate language for having divided things thus, for having separated that which has no need or desire to be separate, and which is of the body to begin with.

...

With you, I am suspect, here in this theatre.

...

The (de)composition of death is (also) a theatre of war. What are we waiting for.

...

Now that these deaths have surfaced, I feel as though I have committed a terrible error, and whatever I do, it is the same death, the same city, the same maniacal expectancy.

...

In Sarah Kane's *Crave*, when C declares "You're dead to me," C is addressing the void left by the voice as much as the hollow of writing. This sentence isn't at all annunciatory; it knows itself to be defeated. The present as it is deployed is a past present, the linguistic theatre gathers into itself the brutality of a past time that is still current. It is over-past, outlasted, replete. Disavowed avowal, of the order of the fait accompli, it remains nonetheless a word (insult) pronounced in the astonishment of devastation, the awareness of the anticipated obsolescence by which it is averted.

...

It rains on all these lives.

...

2004. I left. I didn't try to find out who was stiffening

beneath the blanket, dying, so to speak, exposed. I plugged my ears when the friend who was housing me confirmed this to be a sure sign of my survival. I yelled at the travel agent to get me out of there. I took my legs and ran through all of Barcelona it seemed, which was now comprised of impasses, no more admired Gaudí, no more museus, no more barri Gòtic, young anarchists, dancers in the public squares and the birds I don't forget either. I forget nothing of that which is consigned to forgetting.

...

If there is a concordance between the place of birth and the place of death.

...

The English conceals an aberrant mistranslation. The first feeling is one of shame and irresponsibility. This feeling persists. But alongside it, the further I delve into the misconduct of my line, the more evident it becomes that the literality that usurped my translation is (also) the undigestibility of this death—death's unaccountability, as it were. That the mouth as it is being smothered simply denies the passage to the tongue. Thus do the roses beat clumsily against the ear that mishears.

...

It's summer. The city fires cold.

...

Nor which are the locations, the settings, the capitals or the continents where you cried out the passion of lovers. (Duras)

...

I can do nothing, alas, against such anatomies.

...

Chicago, empty, it's past midnight, a family from Atlanta clutches its suitcases in the train. The mother asks whether I am not afraid, all alone, she repeats, alone, all alone, in the city. No, I say, no, no.

...

And you in the trees with the birds and that terrible number, the enumeration of places.

...

—but it's no use writing by hand, my wrists will break off with my sentences.

...

I might say this to *Look // dead boy* and again to the unfound-hidden. I might say (we had the same *br-----*). And this past tense would betray so much, would consign us each to a kind of death I don't wish to impute to you, because I have met you and you are so alive.

...

(It occurs to me now that I am writing you from the stairwell at the Thin Man in Denver, between the men's room and the door while someone is trying to have a conversation with me about translation. I am not listening, I am writing you, but the voice carries on).

...

Next I want to write : *I was never anyone's lover.*

...

When I leave Chicago, there will only be this: me leaving. Accompanied or unaccompanied, I will take the wheel of the truck and the road will trail off behind me.

…

When I was small I wanted to go unnoticed. I might regret this wish now. Now sometimes I would like it if someone would stand between me and the door and say: stay. But there is hardly a door anymore.

…

It is possible that the problem of narrative resembles the problem of nomination. It's too easy to lean on that armature. But bodies bleed, and who will want for that knowledge – // I am mistaken. It isn't the knowledge that is disastering, but the blood itself, and us with it.

…

Ich war nicht eine Lieberhaber.

…

(Please, correct my German).

…

You're right, we should spend all our Sundays together, and our Fridays and Saturdays, because Friday is always J. beaten at the foot of the building, Saturday is the painter howling through the night, and Sunday, the market, the new moon and his own end, coagulated in my eyes my mouth my hair.

...

Kafka: *as if the shame of it must outlive him*. Which splits open the whole question of the after of writing, of the person who is writing, not as a spectre, but as residue, remains. It is possible that the paradox of surviving (oneself) is in survival itself. Writing is what consigns to that past life, past living—past in the sense of a time past life—such that the fact of surviving (oneself) gives one back to the present—

...

It is this that I hold in my hands, which are not unbruised either, and like most hands, they are simply at the ends of my arms, with my wrists, hold this *nicht-Brief*, this *Schatten*, this *Unerkannt*, this *Freundschaft*, this *Vertrauen*,

...

This postscript has delayed the sending of this *Brief*. Der Brief das ist ein Brief? I will not be so presumptuous! A page slid between days, between a letter and its signature, both between and after.

...

Translation is a form of seduction, and to receive oneself while being received in the language of an other—another language—introduces into the body an abundance of fluctuations that simultaneously bespeak expectancy and the unexpected.

...

In my letter to you, a page has gone missing. It is the same page in every letter, the one that responds. And so this is a kind of post-script embedded in the body of this text. Perhaps it is illegible. Perhaps it is never written. Another form of after-text. Oblivion. Which is another aspect, perhaps, of your unfound-hidden.

...

A body that no longer knows what a body is.

...

I note that I do not know how to write anymore. That

what, of writing, persists, is a remainder of writing, just like the body is but a remainder of living.

...

It is only when I pronounce it out loud, this name Cohen, with its carefully detached syllables, Coh-enne, at the moment at which I am asked to confirm F.'s birth name that the embedded Enne strikes my eyes, my ears, even my fingers register the contact with the sound by a faint shiver, I give a slight cough, that's the expression, which is in poor taste, this nervous giving of a slight cough in the hollow of the brow the word as far as the eye can see, an unlimited name which catches me in the snare once more of descendency. I descend from it, from this Coh-enne starved of my N. on which I insist to the point of disappearance, a nothingness given to disturbance.

...

I say this to you, I wanted only to tell it to you. After I wanted to cover myself over, maybe even hurt myself, just a bit, for having been and not been, that; as though it confirmed both my non-existence and my fault. You see that this has no bearing, all the time spent waiting by the door.

...

—lavender, hops, rushes, ears of wheat, Chinese lanterns, China tree branches, sunflower petals, at the foot of the larch—

...

At ten to one I leave the museum which is on the verge of being engulfed by a wave of women, all roughly the same age, a third age say, and they are invading Michigan Avenue from the north and the south and unfurling like a school of yelping fish from Adams and Monroe on the stairs just as I eject myself, unbreathing, from the building, from Matisse 13–19, his drawings of Tangiers and the melted-burst of blue, slide along the side, insulted in the street to which I concede, and past the Federal Building, just across from the Calder sculpture, before allowing myself to be devoured by the El, the city projects the same vertigo that New York usually reserves for me, and I understand without deference, without distance or dismay, with everything that's left in me of aplomb and stupefaction, that it's over, the city, the emotion, the granite museum you once dreamed, the horror has become irrevocably installed in the self that allows itself to be pushed aside, beyond the edge of the platform, past the rail, nothing to prevent me anymore, no more railing, nor the rail, in fact,

...

If I write it down it's because I don't want to have to say it.

...

The trees are all in flower. I cross the boulevard and I only notice it today. I noticed that I didn't see spring coming. With each tree I relearn the flowers, spring, the redirection of the season. I walk, I don't cry, and then I cry. I stop before the lilacs before returning to my boxes, I note once more that of all of this I am able to retain not a single scent, I live in a state of stupefaction and submersion that prevents me from being in the present, or which makes of the present a drain. It is perhaps in the sense of Madeleine (*Savannah Bay*) that I am living: "If I died, everybody would die, so... it isn't real..." For there to be a world without death, must the world first be denied?

...

Two days and then just one. I don't like this countdown; as for the flowers, they are countless.

...

(*Devastation is belated*)

...

Believe me when I say that Chicago hurts too much,

despite the trees in bloom, the illuminated boulevards. It hurts and I walk just the same, I lift and put down what must be carried, I open the door and close it again, I say nothing of the pitching and tossing, I await the improbable fall, but the sidewalk doesn't seek out my skull, so I walk a bit further. I don't vomit and I don't reject the narrative of the man on the subway platform—his imprisoned nephew, his childhood on the street, his mother's cornbread made of Crisco and Vaseline, the Kalishnikov found by the cops in the back of the truck, the $100,000 bail, and his tears, the young black men who disappear in the murderous fury of spring. That too is a life, that tarmac, the stupefied emotion, I say nothing, I listen, shake his hand. After, it's the platform again, another station, I go. I tell myself that the death I carry is nothing besides, that we are in the same death anyway, and it lurks in the same sun that terrorised Camus, that too, that mortal death from the balconies of the nineteenth century and the rows of abattoirs we walk past.

...

Please forgive me, it's raining.

...

I would like to write you the letter of that duration, but I am so stunned that I can only *imagine* the letter, tossed about as I am by these sorrows sometimes a strange euphoria. Tonight it is a sorrow and it is as vast as this city and installed at my centre. I can only look around me at these boxes and crawl across this floor before surrendering to the day's ending. // I look at the horizon and I cannot distinguish the sky from the floor.

...

The tear is in stead, but I won't make an equation out of it.

...

Today I am unspeakable, that's not right, but I'll say it anyway, language has no need for me.

...

...Dreams, vaguely, very faint, abominable, an immense airport, what else, my bag rolls along without me, I lose the person I am travelling with, a friend hangs up on me, the shower is outside, suspended from the wall of the building, I can't seem to get it to work, my mother emerges through a door on a lower level, far below, and explains the shower, the friend is in bed, I don't hear but I sense his discontent, in the airport there is running, an emergency, identified, none of these things amount to a cataclysm, but that is what it is and it is that by which I wake...

...

...and yet yes, a body, there is a body, carried with difficulty by two people, a dead body, first through one door, then another, they disappear with the body, they leave, they are gone, after they are there again, it is the same body, I confirm, dead, it wasn't dead to begin with, first there is a person, then a dead body, the carriers of the dead don't know it either, they think they are saving a person, I watch as they do, it enters, it goes out, the dead body is so big, so heavy, a leg drags, the carriers are incapable, they pass through one door, the other door, glasses askew...

...

It is not possible to enjoy the theatre without also enjoying boredom. (Brigitte Salino)

...

A person, the dead.

...

The swinging door.

...

...now I am hurtling down a hill, but by what mode of

transportation, I don't know, a horse climbs the hill, shows me his teeth, I should be afraid but he doesn't hurt me when I extend a hand to stroke his face, a woman in an alley, a countryside, we are in front of a little window, in a barn or a bunker, cement walls, underground, there are stairs to get us out of there, but we stop before a small window dug into the wall, the sill is stuffed full of garbage, with my sister, we remove the garbage in order to insinuate ourselves, there is a field, a field between the sick-room and the toppling city...

...

I am torn from it by a will greater than the dream but it's the same guilt, the same fear, the same day begun, and I don't know where it is, urgently, I do not know.

...

I don't speak your name.

...

The photograph: an assumption.

...

No, the sum of the assumption is precisely that in which

it does not respond. Its mechanism is the strike. Its wager is numeral. If I make you into an example, I am failing at my fervour and your discretion. Words like dignity or courage are terrifyingly imprecise; there is not, in the error of vitality, anything besides stupefied idiocy. Admit that that is what pain is made of. It has no morality. It is abject. It remains to be seen upon what surface one must lie, into what hand one must vomit, in what mouth one must fail. It's no longer a dream but a sterile gaze that falls faltering.

...

Howling, besides.

...

Together, now we are together, without.

...

Thank you for these books which will help me to move through the door.

...

Yesterday, for example, as I left the apartment on Chabot, the Berber bakery was closed and I could see the mountain (which isn't really a mountain) in the distance, and there was mist and the trees were in bloom at the back balcony and now I think that's all there is. This end-of-the-world, this sky, this nothing and this horror gathered into me. Does this make me the repository?

...

I thought it in French, or in some approximation of that language.

...

... for I am not convinced I write in any language, nor even that this language is capable of expressing both my disorientation and my effusion. I must be half asleep, but not dreaming, please, not that.

...

Because the *sommes* is as much the exigency of the collective, relational being—nous sommes—as it is the imperative that calls one to the affective order of language—*nous somes sommés, sommées*. To be attentive to the tide that founds and founders being, in other words the eventuality of its *ex-istere*, its situation.

...

Not *death*, but *agony*.

...

I draw the curtain. I draw the curtain and I think: I am drawing the curtain. I make this proposition. We lived here for a time. The sum of the living-here is not calculable. Sooner or later we lie down. There are blinds or a curtain or nothing, for example, no covering. We lie down uncovered, the window there. I am not in time anymore. I demand the abrogation of the time in which we are. It wasn't for reasons of citizenship or settlement. The formal demand is made naturally, in other words in the time in which it is agreed upon. If we howled, together or apart, the howl is presently enclosed in our voices. I say we because I am mistaking myself for a person. A howl that undoes a face.

...

Of course I am incapable of looking, touching, I feel responsible for this thing, and thus, refutable. Astounded. That I did this. Because the doing consolidates something that probably frightens me. It is in this that generosity disappears. *I did this.* You did it too and now we are complicit in this doing. You gave me something, how awkward it all is.

...

The lowest of the low is the count undone. It is the irrefutable summary the sum of which is incalculable.

...

However much one attempts to calculate all the cells in the body, it remains nonetheless that in the end, there is you across from me, our eyes cast aside.

...

Tomorrow I will read in Chicago for the last time. I will empty my voice out.

...

Disgust at the man who avoids the dying friend only to attend the funeral, claiming his time. Me, I.

...

, pain offers itself as a solution to pain, like a second love. (Duras)

...

There is nothing aleatory about Chicago, it is a city that shows itself. But it will mark me as it has marked me, violently and in the unconditional time of smothered avowals. Simply we find that we suddenly have nothing left to say to one another. And so we say this nothing and it is by this nothing that we take our leave.

...

I will speak these words, or will force them out of me and no one will receive them. There is the door by which I enter and the door by which I leave. I have a hard time imagining it, all of it, even at the moment at which it is taking place, has already taken place.

...

It's hard to believe that all of this could happen, that all of this did happen. You see, I have as much difficulty composing my time. But I don't care, because pain is of the present, and it is the very present of removal.

...

The literal body on the verge of detaching itself from its substance, agonising, it knows itself, and knowing itself, undoes.

...

I don't know what discourse will spare us from the pain that drives one into concrete, nor whether pain ought to be spared, but I know what it is to not want or be able to pull oneself out.

...

Pleasure taken in language is already a betrayal of suffering.

...

It's your voice that reads the text to me and stitched into it is J.'s agony, and it is this which wants not to be worded, in the bend, the hitch, the burn, the kill. Because I have come to think of death as murder, and our complicity. // You are right that this is no beginning, it is end upon end,

...

Clearly everything is disproportionately signified at present.

...

If there had been a phone, I would have called to tell you,

called you in the night, say, it seemed the sort of thing one could wake a friend for, imagine waking someone in the night with news like this instead of all the mid-night calls to my sister, to M., over the past three years, the middles of the nights of horror, the gashing of days (and gash, in French, gâcher, is to spoil), *lieber B.*, just writing you awakens parts of me, and I don't intend this to elicit an urgency to respond, simply, imagine this as my mid-night call to you, this, this is you, and how extraordinary, that you do this.

...

I place the stone upon the ground, I make the ground into a mortuary. I pour the pebbles into the lake, I make the lake into a fountain.

...

, as though some vital thing and familiar and strange still subsisted, on the verge of arriving.

...

Now I give myself over to the vertiginous pitching of the continents.

...

The hideous deformity of the self.

...

I watch the door. First the entrance then the exit. Someone berates me for not speaking. But everything has been said. The place anticipates the instance of a body in a place. Speaking is mere consolation. It is much worse than a name, the call.

...

How stupid to think oneself moveable, we don't move, we are nailed to the mouths of others.

...

I realise, walking in this city, that I am waiting for someone to pick me up, like a piece of garbage.

...

To live one's difference to excess.

...

I open the box and I am overcome with disappointment. The same books as before. The books that taught me desire. That gave me what is taken away. I take *The Thirtieth Year* and lock myself in the bedroom. I set fire to the rest.

...

But tell me, is not every gesture accomplished in the very error of the gesture?

...

Yes, the art books, me, a murderer. Une meurtrière. Which is also a tiny slit cut into a wall to see, no doubt obliquely. To see would then mean to kill.

...

I realise too late that the sum is not what remains but that which is removed. This book before me is the sum of all the abandoned books. In sum is one way to disgorge oneself.

...

I bid you farewell. It was I who shouted out. (Bachmann)

...

I am not able to arrive; there is a shame in the place of my having come here.

...

No, it isn't finished. There's more to hear, hear the voice, the questions, encourage oneself, protect oneself, struggle as well to go all the way to the end, with that immense cowardice of preferring words, their edifice, to the small inconceivable, gesture, that I am not yet able to make. (Collobert)

...

The painter loved this blue he said cobalt, night falling, a fallen blue?

...

To be in the voice before, the voice before the body, the voice of the body that does not lean against speaking but endeavours to live in the present with its sorrows and lurches.

...

Chicago had been a sort of wild forest.

...

A hideous howl pulls me from sleep, I wake by this howl. A dune, a house, birds decorated with martial feathers, animals—horses?—decorated as well, it is a dune and also a plain, neighbours whose wall touches mine. A deep wall that descends beneath the earth where the arrangement of space recalls other places, a library, a forbidden place. There is A., then S., the parents, a rag, a map of Chicago pinned to the wall, laughter, it is stained, laughter that is even more quiet, gently, we speak in quiet, your traces on this bit of fabric, I want to go up, out, up, but the way goes lower, bamboo, hardwood, A. sits down, there is the stranger who meets me, we meet in the dunes, we cross over, the other side with the decorated birds, the horses, a grave silence, we entwine, first in the bamboo of a kitchen installed beneath the earth, then on that dune, let's go, I say, we go, walk in the astonishment of walking, our bodies touch, I turn, the wave rises, throws me onto the side with the birds, the horses, the stranger, swallowed by the wave risen from the depth of every ocean, cry, I cry out, a howl that runs after the body, plunges into my stomach, I open my eyes, gutted,

...

Nor the present.

...

340

If I wanted, I could pass for a child of forty years of philosophy. (Duras)

...

I understand that I don't exist, here or anywhere. I understand the degree to which the road is vacant even when it is crowded. I understand that I am killing myself as much as everyone around me.

...

Forgive me this letter. I miss you. I read you, there is a sharp pain in my chest, like the time last week when we spoke, and so I think that I must be a murderer of sorts, a murderer of people and of cities.

...

I could go back. I tell myself this. Then I tell myself that I'd be better off drowning in the ocean.

...

He says that there is hope. I say no, there is no hope. That hope always rests on a future that doesn't arrive; a future with no concordance in the present. That hope must be of the present otherwise it is not hope, it is life forever postponed in favour of derailing hopefulness. He says okay hope in the present, a present tied to a vow, a belief. As you like, I say to him, except there is no present either.

...

Among all the books, there is a great thirst.

...

What will be said of me, that I was intolerant, maladapted, and frankly indefensible, she thought she was a boy, she never did extract herself from her story, she closed everything, even her name in the end she remained caught in it.

...

Now I will sleep against the continent that does not dream says nothing wanders off among the acacias like the giraffes in the very tall book from a time before the wretched time that was predicted in the forty years to come.

...

That blood may be the carrier of a culture, as of an illness. So what.

...

The space of address is indicated by a blank. Un blanc, which is a space, the colour white, and a blank, in an arsenal of false attempts at murder. Still, they have been known to kill.

...

Two weeks or so since my transport here. I don't quite know what word to attach to it, I am even more distrustful than usual, of words that encircle a place, tender a distance, put an end.

...

Thus do I no longer invent your story.

...

And if I look at my paltry recent attempts at communication with people, the notes I've made with very little conviction in the current notebook, I see that the word *murder* appears again and again: But it made me feel once again like The Murderer. // ...and so here is another opportunity for me to feel like I've committed a murder. // Je n'en peux plus d'être le meurtrier. // ...so much that it seems I've committed a murder by coming here. // ...and so I think that I must be a murderer of sorts, a murderer of people and of cities. // Because I have come to think of death as murder, and our complicity.—This is quite the tribunal. And I am made curious by it as I collect together these propositions, but I am made to do this by the quick sense of culpability upon reading your most recent brief, in which your own grief is invigorated by mine, and I want to remove this somehow; I don't want to be the conduit to other devastations. And yet it seems each time that I am; it is possible now that I am only this, in Chicago and in Montréal.

...

I am not sure what age this is. For myself, I will be forty in a month. Forty, which has become the age of death. I proposed to a friend that to mark the occasion we set fire to the mountain.

...

Le désastre est séparé, ce qu'il y a de plus séparé. (Blanchot)— *Disaster is separate; that which is most separate.* (Interesting here, Smock's insertion of the semi-colon, making more distinct the *separation* between clauses). This separateness (se-par-tition) may not then (or not only) be what is not us, but also what happens (to us) without announcing itself; is the unpreparedness in disaster itself, or in our coming to disaster? In disaster's coming at (to) us? Surely its separateness must also be in its inability to be languaged. In this strange logic, the outsider is also the disaster but only because it is given to this in thought. Our (human) fixation on limits, borders, boundaries, confines, must surely be embedded in a profound anxiety as to the impossibility of such. Which brings me to want to wonder about disaster and proximity, disaster and intimacy, and whether there can be intimacies in disaster, among disasters, and if these proximities cease to be intimacies at all precisely because of the *a priori* separations of which Blanchot speaks.

...

After the fire there will be several days more at this table, some walking in this city, and the next city, which will be yours.

...

I say letter of this letter, but I can never really be sure. Maybe a letter, instead of being separate from the other forms, is the place where many forms meet. This must be so, since it is a space of encounter, which makes possible encounter — which, if you'll allow one more etymological indulgence— comes from the Old French *encontre,* a hermaphroditic word, *m.* or *f.*—

...

Neuter, it is said, but neuter is without desire.

...

But encounter is itself disastrous. One of the acceptions of the French *rencontre* is combative and refers to the massacre of animals (pronounced prey in order to dispense with any ethical consideration; as one says of the pig, pork, of cows, cattle, of chickens, poultry). The *rencontre* is also the animal head nailed to the wall of the lodge, the display of successive *slaughters*. Such that encounter, such as Buber envisioned it, and which Lévinas pursued, is always already a form of *putting to death*. *To see* would thus mean *to kill*.

...

Capsized in this city. Tossed about on an ocean that doesn't arrive.

...

It's the *return* which is confusing. The overlay of the place of birth on the place of ---vival, is unheard of. For it is not, properly speaking, a return. I don't know what word to put there. It's *there is* conjugated with *there was*. The *not* is missing.

...

Love from this rue Chabot where the gulls have found the sky's anticipated sea.

...

I rearrange the chairs. I remove the armchair. The other one, however, the green one, painted with four hands, I carry all the way here as well as the rope that attaches the arm that is coming off. Shortly after I arrive, I take two white chairs onto my back, wooden chairs, even though in principle I don't like painted wood, one day and then the next, one white chair and then the next, at the entrance, I leave the chairs there, latent chairs, I say, that haven't assumed their function as chairs, but hold their place. The chairs are all empty and yet as soon as I arrive it's impossible to sit down, the two cats occupy the twelve chairs including the bed.

...

The living might do well to remain near their dead. It is perhaps in this that the Moderns will find the source of our collective hysteria. I am no doubt at fault for being far from the river that imbibed the remains of my creatures, and the lake across from the nuclear plant replete with a painter's ashes, at fault for planting gardens and bringing my body closer to a breath.

...

In the absence of a conversation, of a place which concedes a self, one must substitute a self invented against and despite the structures of denial erected against it. But once the challenge has been met, one must also know how to leave; there is no point prolonging one's suffering.

...

For nothing, I would say.

...

...if the horse lies down to sleep, will it choke in the fog? (Yuriy Norshteyn)

...

I had wanted not to have (been) detached. I had wanted for a proximity.

...

In the Sisyphus text, there is talk of murder.

...

In this sense, these texts are distinct from earlier work, though this sort of distinction is no doubt futile; one is never as far from oneself as one would like to believe.

...

In 1944 there was already Shostakovich. In the notes accompanying the sonata for viola and piano, I catch in passing 'a more private grief'. And when I read: 'the extreme pain in Shostakovich's composing hand,' I don't anticipate the poliomyelitis, but another, far less literal pain. (What is a literal pain). The private voice of the viola always recalls Gorecki's *en dehors*. When I bought this record, the bookseller asked whether I was a violist. Just like last year when the bookseller asked whether I was Spinozist as I was buying his *Ethics*, which remains just as unreadable. No, and I am not one of those travellers who arrives either. I am nothing of that which you suspect, nothing. Even less so than usual.

...

I am freshly annihilated, and yet, this morning, I must learn not to say and yet, c'est fini. The birds fly into the trees. Where are my eyes.

...

My circulation seems utterly interrupted, like the train

between Nice and Toulon. Must we rush off to the Var, settle in Draguignan and wait for the waters to come down? In 2007, there were the fires of Antibes. There is this word, *calm*, indecipherable. Calumny, yes.

...

When I die, it's hardly likely that someone will write a quartet dedicated to my memory. So I decided to write it myself. One could write on the frontispiece, "Dedicated to the author of this quartet." (Dmitri Shostakovitch)

...

Please forgive all the time it has taken for me to write. I was seized by a kind of muteness and the rain doesn't stop. So I listen to Hindemith, and count the minutes between extremities.

...

All around there is an emptiness. It is easy enough to leap into the void, to go off in all directions, east, south, head on.

...

Certainly do not congratulate yourself for a life before having lived it.

...

Wears white in times of rain.

...

I lied, I opened your letter before sleep; I am breaking almost all my rules, there are books in the bedroom and clothes on the kitchen counter and tools on my work-table and mail just about everywhere.

...

Gefühl.

...

(...now there is the grief of Schnittke...)

...

You are the only one to answer to my name of Nathanaël.

...

The message states: *votre envoi a été supprimé*. Of this I retain the *voi* of *envoi*, surrendering thus to my muteness.

...

It is in this that the question of concordance is of interest, because it is a false question. The coincidence of N. and this birthplace is in a sense an anomaly, not at all a *return* toward a place, but simply a *going-there*.

...

I arrive and I undo. I undo, not in order to place but to remove. Irigaray, for example, I remove. Immediately, I remove Irigaray and Bachelard and Benedict Anderson and others yet which I stuff onto the shelf in the closet with the plate from Greece and the inline skates. I am drawing up an inventory in reverse. I am emptying the place.

...

Zero is the equivalent of the letter *e*.

...

Thus do I invent the itinerary of others.

...

It happens that people gather around a word. Love, for example. They empty out the place of their being to enter into that pronunciation.

...

Are we dying, M., that must be it, dying face first in close-up.

...

It doesn't matter, it's just a face, and no one really seems to see it.

...

Minha amiga, where are we now? This is today's rainstorm from my study window. It echoes the storm inside—familiar, to you no doubt, all day a howl in my head, and I am barely emerged from it. I rode twenty kilometres on my bike and imagined a thousand escape routes back to Chicago. Ready to empty out this place and hurtle back to the lake, the river, and M. with his walking. And then what? It hurts to be anywhere. It hurts to have left. I don't know what violence I've done nor to whom. I watch the storm and am buried in ash. It's all gone. I think I'll go mad with it, R., what else is there left to do but to go mad? I stare at the tall young Mexican man at the raw food kiosque and just want him to hit me. And then I walk out with my change and it's another waste of time. No one wants to look at this face with these eyes which are too wide and too slow and too stupid to even know what a world is. It can be like that. But I hope you will forgive me this letter and tell me how you are.

...

It's possible that I have come here to lose my head. Once I will have finished losing my head I will leave again, with neither head nor place.

...

The word *crime* is just, and I couldn't say who of Cain or Abel was wrong, nor whether a name is capable of settling a death. I touched the very skin of that death, and it has stayed with me. With flight, there is also the doorstep.

...

M. is an engineer; in this, as far as I am concerned, he is a great poet, a great philosopher.

...

Your voice arrived from a terribly intimate part of your body, this is as I heard it, I feel it now, in my own body, in a part that didn't exist before our speaking just now.

...

Having reached the end of the world, what choice does one have but to retrace one's steps.

...

Hurl oneself at the void.

...

Me, I think that I am falling. There is this: fall. I am mistaken. After death, one looks everywhere for death, it is everywhere desired, even as it is disavowed.

...

I open the book in the rain. I place the stones against the rail.

...

Necessity must be in madness.

...

Others say it and then I say it. After I think that it was I who said it and I have no idea where it comes from.

...

Thursday forty years. The painter's last age.

...

It is but the facsimile of a life, with neither substance nor form, in this place which could belong to no one.

...

Here trying to put an end. Resolutely empty. Saw the Xenakis. Everything in fits and starts. I read very little. Don't write. Cannot say of this: living. Have lost all of my distances. City that lies to me.

...

But B., the writer is the executioner. We do this.

...

This summer will have taken the form of a decision.

...

It really is the end of a world, and I feel as though I am posted in Siberia or Singapore, in a strange sing-songy compound where the children carry guns in the form of balloons but the next boat out of here isn't for another month.

...

You leave and I don't cry. For eight months I cry and then I don't cry. I say a thing I don't hear myself saying and you answer.

...

A geometry that might be qualitative.

...

It's there, in your voice.

...

On my fortieth birthday, as I was crossing the demarcation line clandestinely with the black cat, I wished I had been born the day before. (Malraux)

...

It isn't because it is there that it must of necessity be confronted. And it may be true that the confrontation is in fact in the deviation. Which is not the same thing as an escape. Nor a disappointment.

...

As for me I am writing the ends at present, not conclusions, but lasts. And these are in accordance with an inability—a refusal—both of the au-revoir and the arrival. There was no saying good-bye to the painter. At the moment at which the end seemed to announce itself rapidly, the ends simply accumulated, and we threw ourselves from end to end, him at his easel, me in the city, tugging at spare parts, and even the last gasp was astonishingly (a)live. The doors opened and closed so many times that they ceased to be doors.

...

I am lying at least a little bit, because I am not writing at all this summer, besides these letters which are less and less letters, but something else much less accountable.

...

On Bernard, I glimpse the painter in the body of a man.

...

It's impossible, and I carry a sort of terror or detachment, a retinal disturbance that superimposes forms and moments. For now I want to reach Chicago again where I have the mad hope of reintegrating a life, instead of this unfounded suspension.

...

It is possible that it is everywhere the same, this wanderment, this lack, this seizure of the body overhanging a sort of precipice. But perhaps it is I who invented the precipice, as well as the body.

...

Every language is provincial, every human is mediocre. Every work, a form of massacre.

...

The apprenticeship of the provisional.

...

Does it ever occur to psychoanalysis to say no? It seems to me just as important to recognise the hidden text as it is to resolve not to read it.

...

It is obvious now that everything is provisional. Of course, it was always so, but my (somatic) apprehension of it is different. I can only answer for myself. Go toward that which, in me, awaits. At present, it is Chicago. Because the question of this city need not be asked. After, it may be elsewhere again. But I'm not too concerned about that. What comes next will declare itself. I will have made my way. It is in this, no doubt, that I am so well accorded, after all, to this America that I will have spent three quarters of my life execrating.

...

Very early this morning it was a group, first of cyclists wearing yellow jackets, and then a second group, in orange, and it always upsets me to see people organised against their autonomy and I have no doubt already expressed my deep distrust of consensus. Consensus is another manifestation of the crowd and the inoffensive orange vests are not so far, in the end, from the fascist abattoirs.

...

To cross the border toward your country is to leave the body of my sister, to take possession of something that escapes me. But what violence, to tear her body from mine, where it is lodged, with the other bodies gathered there.

...

Photography is the epitome of disavowal. I mean that it is the epitaph. It disavows the line and draws a line. Your face, for example. I don't cry over you but over the summary drawn by the photograph of proximities. The face, say, driven into its pain. And the sense I have of leaving you by my disavowed and disavowing eyes. As though the sense of the eyes rested there were a desistance. Mine first, because I am the one looking, and then the one who doesn't arrive.

...

While I am asleep next to you, I dream that you are far. You send me paper letters that arrive in the form of SMS's. I am being over-looked.

...

It's time. I will have survived the blueberries, but barely. In the seasons it's true there is the lure of a kind of expiation. But it isn't that at all. It's simply that the blueberries will have given amply of themselves. And like the blueberries, Montréal, and my bicycle. I placed green tea compresses on the eyes of the cat and immediately, the pain subsided. That the body of an animal.

...

Last night we said too much, and the wine – the same pinot gris as the first time. And I drank of that wine and defended positions that are no longer mine. A weariness settled in. We ate the last blueberries and B. fell asleep while S. lit and relit her cigar. Me, I stopped talking, and quietly I left.

...

In a box, I find some ferrotypes as well as a photograph dated March 4, 2005. One month before Chicago.

...

R.: It is my want that it is looked at closely and in light, please.

...

Must I be the one to survive, not only the book, but never?

...

I'm reading André Bazin. The charge of the thing interposed between thing and thing speaks at length of the so-called human being's need to be subtracted from a situation, to surrender emotion.

...

...the brutal certainty that I was never there last year when everything was stopping. And the fear of not having, of not having been able, and let it all escape, of having committed the fault of condemnable lack of attention, while M. was face to face, he was able to say: at (the) last.

...

Tomorrow I will take my bicycle, and mend the flaked edge of the lake.

...

At night I open the curtains, to let the light in.

Chicago, Montréal, Chicago
2009–2010, November

, there is emptiness or interment, so I walk, not outside nor in

Middle Summaries

Discord   Etel Adnan, *Of Cities & Women (Letters to Fawwaz)*,
Sausalito, The Post-Apollo Press, 1993.

Giorgio Agamben, *The Coming Community*, tr. Michael
Hardt, Minneapolis, University of Minnesota, 1990.

Diana Agrest et al., *The Sex of Architecture*, New York,
Harry N. Abrams, 1996.

Jean Améry, *At the Mind's Limits*, tr. Sidney Rosenfeld and
Stella P. Rosenfeld, New York, Schocken, 1986.

Claude Arnaud, *Qui dit je en nous?* Paris, Grasset, 2006.

V.I. Arnold, *Catastrophe Theory*, tr. R. K. Thomas, Berlin,
Heidelberg, New York, Tokyo, Springer-Verlag, 1984.

Ingeborg Bachmann, *Leçons de Francfort*, tr. Elfie Poulain,
Arles, Actes Sud, 1986; *Malina*, tr. Philippe Jaccottet,
Paris, Seuil, 1973.

Roland Barthes, *Le degré zéro de l'écriture*, Paris, Seuil,
1953 et 1972.

Georges Bataille, *La haine de la poésie*, Paris, Minuit, 1947;
L'impossible, Paris, Minuit, 1962; *Madame Edwarda, Le
mort, Histoire de l'œil*, Paris, 10/18, 1967.

Simone de Beauvoir, *Pyrrhus et Cinéas*, Paris, Gallimard, 1944.

Walter Benjamin, *Écrits français*, Paris, Gallimard, 1991.

Joseph Beuys, *Par la présente, je n'appartiens plus à l'art*,
Paris, L'Arche, 1988.

Yves Bonnefoy, *Une autre époque de l'écriture*, Paris, Mercure
de France, 1988.

Nina Bouraoui, *Garçon manqué*, Paris, Stock, 2000.

Pierre-Alain Buhler, *La Wue, La Mue*, Paris, des femmes, 1983.

Cabinet Magazine, no. 10 (2006).

Albert Camus, *Le mythe de Sisyphe*, Paris, Gallimard, 1942.

Patrick Chamoiseau, Édouard Glissant. *Quand les murs tombent : l'identité nationale hors-la-loi?*, Paris, Galaade Institut du Tout-Monde, 2007.

René Char. *Feuillets d'Hypnos*. Paris, Gallimard, 1946.

Victor Chklovski, *La marche du cheval*, tr. Michel Pétris, Paris, Champ Libre, 1973.

E.M. Cioran, *Précis de Décomposition*, Paris, Gallimard, 1949.

Collectif, *La vie à en mourir : Lettres de fusillés (1941– 1944)*, s.l., Éditions Tallandier, 2006 (2003).

Danielle Collobert, *Œuvres I et II*, Paris, P.O.L., 2004 et 2005.

Le Corbusier, *La Ville Radieuse (éléments d'une doctrine d'urbanisme pour l'équipement de la civilisation machiniste)*, Paris, Éditions Vincent, Fréal & Cie, 1964 (1933).

Jacques Derrida, *Donner la mort*, Paris, Galilée, 1999; *Chaque fois unique, la fin du monde*, Paris, Galilée, 2003; *Apprendre à vivre enfin*, Paris, Galilée, 2005.

Assia Djebar, *Le blanc de l'Algérie*, Paris, Albin Michel, 1995; La disparition de la langue française, Paris, Albin Michel, 2003.

Marguerite Duras et Xavière Gauthier, *Les Parleuses*, Paris, Minuit, 1974; *Sublime, forcément sublime Christine V.*, précédé de *Duras Aruspice* de Catherine Mavrikakis, Montréal, Héliotrope, 2008; *Cahiers de la guerre et autres textes*, Paris, P.O.L./Imec, 2006; *Le navire night*, Paris, Mercure de France, 1979; Marguerite Duras et Michelle Porte, *Les lieux de Marguerite Duras*, Paris, Minuit, 1977.

Paul Éluard, *Capitale de la douleur*, Paris, Gallimard, 1926 et 1929.

Lucienne Favre, *Tout l'inconnu de la casbah d'Alger*, Alger, Baconnier Frères, 1933. *France Culture*, Radio France Internationale

Michel Foucault, *L'ordre du discours*, Paris, Gallimard, 1970.

Édouard Glissant, *L'intention poétique*, Paris, Seuil, 1969.

Noah Eli Gordon et Joshua Marie Wilkinson, *Figures for a Darkroom Voice*, Townshend (VT), Tarpaulin Sky Press, 2007.

Hervé Guibert, *À l'ami qui ne m'a pas sauvé la vie*, Paris, Gallimard, 1990.

Martin Heidegger, *La dévastation et l'attente, Entretien sur le chemin de campagne*, tr. Philipps Arjakovksy et Hadrien France-Lanord, Paris, Gallimard, 2006.

Thierry Hentsch, *La mer, la limite*, préface de Suzanne Jacob, Montréal, Héliotrope, 2006.

Guy Hocquenghem, *L'amphithéâtre des morts*, Paris, Gallimard, 1994.

Eugène Ionesco, *Présent passé, Passé présent*, Paris, Mercure de France, 1968; *Journal en miettes*, Paris, Mercure de France, 1967.

Edmond Jabès, *Le petit livre de la subversion hors de soupçon*, Paris, Gallimard, 1982.

Suzanne Jacob, *Histoires de s'entendre*, Montréal, Boréal, 2008; *Fugueuses*, Montréal, Boréal, 2005.

Vladimir Jankélévitch, *Pardonner?*, Paris, Roger Maria, 1971.

Agota Kristof. *C'est égal*, Paris, Seuil, 2005.

Emmanuel Lévinas, *De l'évasion*, Paris, Fata Morgana, 1982.

Lucy Lippard. *Eva Hesse*. New York, Da Capo Press, 1976 (NYUP)/1992.

Maïakovski, *Vers et Proses*, tr. Elsa Triolet, s.l., Éditeurs français réunis, 1957.

Catherine Mavrikakis, *Omaha Beach: Un oratorio*, Montréal, Héliotrope, 2008.

Kazimir Malevitch, "Suprematism" (1927), tr. Howard Dearstyne, in *Modern Artists On Art*, ed. Robert L. Herbert, Englewood Cliffs, NJ: Prentice-Hall, 1964.

Stéphane Mallarmé, *Pour un tombeau d'Anatole*, Paris, Seuil, 1961.

André Malraux, *Carnets d'URSS* 1934, Paris, Gallimard, 2007; *L'espoir*, Paris, Gallimard, 1937; *La tentation de l'Occident*, Paris, Grasset, 1926.

Mariana Marin, *Paper Children*, tr. Adam J. Sorkin, Brooklyn (NY), Ugly Duckling Presse, 2006.

Maurice Merleau-Ponty, *L'œil et l'esprit*, Paris, Gallimard, 1964.

Jean-Luc Nancy, À *l'écoute*, Paris, Galilée, 2002; *L'intrus*, Paris, Galilée, 2000.

Ernst Reijseger, *Requiem for a Dying Planet*, München, Winter&Winter, 2006.

Denise Riley, *Impersonal Passion*, Duke, 2005.

Simone Weil, *La pesanteur et la grâce*, Paris, Plon, 1947 / 1988.

Spirale Magazine.

N., *Un pigeon meurt sur ma voix*, in *La cendre des mots*, Paris, L'Harmattan, 2003.

Jean-Jacques Rousseau, *Les Confessions*, Paris, Gallimard, 1959.

Nathalie Sarraute, *Entre la vie et la mort*, Paris, Gallimard, 1968; *Isma*, Paris, Gallimard, 1970.

Wallace Stevens, *The Collected Poems of Wallace Stevens*. London: Faber and Faber, 1959.

Michel Tournier, *Célébrations*, Paris, Mercure de France, 1999.

Vladimir Voinovich, *The Ivankiad*, New York, Farrar, Strauss and Giroux, 1976 / 1977.

Virginia Woolf, *The Waves*, San Diego, Harcourt, 1959 (1931).

Kateb Yacine, *Le polygone étoilé*, Paris, Seuil, 1966 / 1994.

Deliberation Diana Agrest, et al., *The Sex of Architecture*, New York, Harry N. Abrams, 1996.

Ingeborg Bachmann, *Leçons de Francfort: Problèmes de poésie contemporaine*, tr. Elfie Poulain, Paris, Actes Sud, 1986.

Walter Benjamin, *Fragments*, tr. Christophe Jouanlanne et Jean-François Poirier, Paris, PUF, 2001 ; *Œuvres III*, tr. Maurice Gandillac, Rainer Rochlitz, Pierre Rusch, Paris, Gallimard, 2000 ; *Selected Writings: Volume I, 1913–1926*, ed. Marcus Bullock, Michael W. Jennings, Cambridge (MA), Belknap, 1996; *Sens unique précédé de Une enfance berlinoise*, tr. Jean Lacoste, s.l., Les Lettres Nouvelles/ Maurice Nadeau, 2007 (1978, 1988).

Simone Benmussa, *Entretiens avec Nathalie Sarraute*, Tournai (Belgique), La Renaissance du Livre, 1999.

Maurice Blanchot, *Une voix venue d'ailleurs*, Paris, Gallimard, 2002.

Marc Bloch, *L'étrange défaite*, Paris, Gallimard, 1990.

Nina Bouraoui, *La Vie heureuse*, Paris, Stock, 2002.

Martin Buber, *Between Man and Man*, London and New York, Routledge, 1947.

Melissa Buzzeo, *Face*, Toronto, BookThug, 2009.

Albert Camus, *Le mythe de Sisyphe*, Paris, Gallimard, 1942.

Claude Cahun, *Aveux Non Avenus*, Paris, Éditions du Carrefour, 1930.

Victor Chklovski, *La marche du cheval*, Paris, Champ Libre, 2003.

Inger Christensen, *alphabet*, tr. Susanna Nied, New York, New Directions, 1981/2000.

Émil Cioran, *De l'inconvénient d'être né*, Paris, Gallimard, 1973.

Hélène Cixous, *Rêve je te dis*, Paris, Galilée, 2003; *Ex-Cities*, Philadelphia, Slought Books, 2005.

René Clément, *La bataille du rail*, 1946.

Mahmoud Darwich, *Une mémoire pour l'oubli*, tr. Yves Gonzales-Quijano and Farouk Mardam-Bey, Paris, Actes Sud, 1994.

Mahmoud Darwish, *Memory for Forgetfulness, August, Beirut, 1982*, tr. Ibrahim Muhawi, Berkeley (CA), University of California Press, 1995.

Dérives, « Autour de Jean-Claude Rousseau », Nº 1-2007.

Jacques Derrida, *Feu la cendre*, Paris, des femmes, 1987; *Éperons les styles de Nietzsche/Spurs Nietzsche's Styles*, tr. Barbara Harlow, London et Chicago, University of Chicago Press, 1978/1979; *Was ist Dichtung?* Berlin, Brinkmann & Bose, 1990; *La vérité en peinture*, Paris, Flammarion, 1978.

Tahar Djaout, *Le dernier été de la raison*, Paris, Seuil, 1999.

Anne Dufourmantelle, *Blind Date: sexe et philosophie*, Paris, Calmann-Lévy, 2003.

Marguerite Duras, *Les Parleuses*, Paris, Minuit, 1974; *Hiroshima mon amour*, Paris, Gallimard, 1960; *L'Éden Cinéma*, Paris, Mercure de France, 1977.

France Culture, 2009.

Sigmund Freud, *Un souvenir d'enfance de Léonard de Vinci*, Paris, Gallimard, 2003.

Asher Ghaffar, *Wasps in a Golden Dream Hum a Strange Music*, Toronto, ECW, 2008.

Hervé Guibert, *Le mausolée des amants*, Paris, Gallimard, 2001.

Harper's Magazine, June 2009.

Martin Heidegger, *What is called thinking?*, tr. J. Glenn Gray, New York, Harper & Row, 1968; *Basic Writings*, multiple tr., New York, HarperSanFrancisco, 2008 (1977).

Hans Höller et al., *Ingeborg Bachmann : Schreiben gegen den Krieg / Writing Against War*, Wien, Löcker, 2008.

Max Horkheimer and Theodor W. Adorno, *La dialectique de la raison*, Paris, Gallimard, 1983.

Elfriede Jelinek, *Einar*, Sausalito (CA), tr. P. J. Blumenthal, Post-Apollo, 2006; *Wonderful Wonderful Times*, tr. Michael Hulse, London, Serpent's Tail, 1990.

Emmanuel Kant, *Sur l'échec de tout essai philosophique en matière de théodicée*, tr. Antoine Grandjean, Paris, Éditions Cécile Defaut, 2009.

Bhanu Kapil, *The Vertical Interrogation of Strangers*, Berkeley (CA), Kelsey Street, 2009 (2001).

Sarah Kane, *Crave*, London, Methuen, 2001.

Imre Kertész, *L'holocauste comme culture*, tr. Natalia

Zaremba-Huzsvai and Charles Zaremba, Arles, Actes Sud, 2009.

Myung Mi Kim, *Dura*, New York, Nightboat, 2008 (1988).

Sarah Kofman, *Camera Obscura. De l'idéologie*, Paris, Galilée, 1973.

Bernard-Marie Koltès, *Récits Morts*, Paris, Minuit, 2008; *Voix sourdes*, Paris, Minuit, 2008; *La fuite à cheval très loin dans la ville*, Paris, Minuit, 1984; *Dans la solitude des champs de coton*, Paris, Minuit, 1986.

Rosalind E. Krauss, *The Originality of the Avant-Garde and Other Modernist Myths*, Cambridge (MA), London, The MIT Press, 1985.

Jacques Lacan, *Écrits II*, Paris, Seuil, 1971.

Sophie Lacroix, *Ruine*, Paris, La Villette, 2008.

René Lapierre, *Traité de physique*, Montréal, Les Herbes Rouges, 2009.

Claude Lanzmann, *Le lièvre de Patagonie*, Paris, Gallimard, 2009.

Michel Lussault, *L'homme spatial*, Paris, Seuil, 2007.

Maïakovski, *Vers et proses*, tr. Elsa Triolet, Éditeurs français réunis, 1957.

Jeff Marlin, *Divergences from vertical*, drawings (pencil on paper), private collection, 2005.

Catherine Mavrikakis, *La mauvaise langue*, Seyssel, Champ de Vallon, 1996.

Patrick Maynard, *The Engine of Visualization: Thinking Through Photography*, Ithaca, Cornell University Press, 1997.

Jean-Luc Nancy, *L' « il y a » du rapport sexuel*, Paris, Galilée, 2001; *L'Intrus*, Paris, Galilée, 2000.

Nathanaël, *At Alberta*, Toronto, BookThug, 2008; in *Spirale*, 2009. "Como los perros de mi sombra," "La mort de son vivant," etc.; *L'absence au lieu (Claude Cahun et le livre inouvert)*, Québec, Nota Bene, coll. Nouveaux Essais Spirale, 2007; *UNDERGROUND*, Laval, TROIS, 1999.

Michel Onfray, *Le songe d'Eichmann*, Paris, Galilée, 2008.

Juhani Pallasmaa, *The Eyes of the Skin: Architecture and the Senses*, Chichester (GB), Wiley, 2005.

Alejandra Pizarnik, *Poesía completa*, ed. Ana Becciu, Barcelona, Editorial Lumen, 2000.

Marcel Proust, *Contre Sainte-Beuve*, Paris, Gallimard, 1954.

Ed Roberson, *City Eclogue*, Berkeley (CA), Atelos, 2006.

Lisa Robertson, *Lisa Robertson's Magenta Soul Whip*, Toronto, Coach House, 2009.

Danièle Sallenave, *Castor de guerre*, Paris, Gallimard, 2008.

Arthur Schopenhauer, *Essai sur le libre arbitre*, tr. Salomon Reinach, Paris, Éditions Rivages, 1992.

Jorge Semprún, *Mal et modernité*, Paris, Climats, 1990, 1995.

William Shakespeare, *Twelfth Night*, London, Penguin Classics, 1968.

Marie-Hélène Vieira da Silva, *Peintures 1935–1969*, catalogue d'exposition, Paris, Musée National d'Art Moderne, 1969.

Zafer Şenocak, *Door Languages*, Brookline (MA), Zephyr Press, 2008.

Several Silences April 26–June 7, 2009, The Renaissance Society, University of Chicago.

Baruch Spinoza, *De la liberté de penser dans un État libre*, Paris, L'Herne, 2007.

Verena Stefan. *D'ailleurs*, tr. Louis Bouchard et Marie-Elisabeth Morf, Montréal, Héliotrope, 2009.

Benjamin Stora, *La gangrène et l'oubli. La mémoire de la guerre d'Algérie*, Paris, Éditions de la Découverte, 1992.

Abdellah Taia, *Une mélancolie arabe*, Paris, Seuil, 2008.

Jun'ichiro Tanizaki, *In Praise of Shadows*, Stony Creek (CT), Leete's Island, 1977.

Paul Virilio, *Bunker Archéologie*, Paris, Galilée, 2008 (1975); *L'accident originel*, Paris, Galilée, 2005.

Krzysztof Warlikowski, *Théâtre écorché*, Arles, Actes Sud, 2007.

John Willett, *Art & Politics in the Weimar Period : The New Sobriety 1917-1933*, New York, Pantheon, 1978.

Sylvia Wolf, *Michal Rovner : The Space Between*, New York, Whitney Museum, 2002.

Summation   Yann Andréa, *M.D.*, Paris, Minuit, 1983.

Rachel Gontijo Araújo, "Primary Anatomy," Action Yes, 2009; *Pornapocalipse*, no pants, 2010.

Ingeborg Bachmann, *The Book of Franza & Requiem for Fanny Goldman*, tr. Peter Filkins, Evanston (IL), Northwestern, 1999; "Fragment d'Anna".

Maurice Blanchot, *Le dernier à parler*, Saint-Clément, Fata Morgana, 1984.

Daniel Canty, in *La Table des Matières*, Le Quartanier, 2007.

René Char, *Fureur et mystère*, Paris, Gallimard, 1962/1967.

Cioran, *La tentation d'exister*, Paris, Gallimard, 1956.

Danielle Collobert, *Œuvres I*, Paris, P.O.L., 2004.

Stig Dagerman, *Notre besoin de consolation est impossible à rassasier*, tr. Ph. Bouquet, Arles, Actes Sud, 1981; *La dictature du chagrin*, Marseille, Agone, 2001 (1999).

Jacques Derrida, *Fichus*, Paris, Galilée, 2002.

Mladen Dolar, *A Voice and Nothing More*, Cambridge (MA), MIT, 2006.

Marguerite Duras, *Savannah Bay*, Paris, Minuit, 1982–1983/2007; *La pluie d'été*, Paris, P.O.L., 1990.

Pierre Fédida, *Des bienfaits de la dépression*, Paris, Odile Jacob, 2001.

Jean Genet, *Œuvres complètes IV*, Paris, Gallimard, 1968; *Haute surveillance*, Paris, Gallimard, 1965.

André Gorz, *Lettre à D.*, Paris, Gallimard, 2006.

Hervé Guibert, *Le mausolée des amants, Journal 1976–1991*, Paris, Gallimard, 2001; *La pudeur ou l'impudeur*, 1991; *Le seul visage*, Minuit, 1984.

Suzanne Hancock, *Cast from Bells*, Montréal, McGill-Queen's, 2010.

Peter Handke, *Kaspar and Other Plays*, tr. Michael Roloff, New York, Farrar, Straus and Giroux, 1969.

Eugène Ionesco, *Journal en miettes*, Paris, Mercure de France, 1967; *Ruptures de silence*, Paris, Mercure de France, 1995.

Bernard-Marie Koltès, *Combat de nègre et de chiens*, Paris, Minuit, 1989.

Jean-François Lyotard, *Chambre sourde: l'antiesthétique de Malraux*, Paris, Galilée, 1993.

André Malraux, *Le Miroir des Limbes I, Antimémoires*, Paris, Gallimard, 1972; *Le Miroir des Limbes II, La corde et les souris*, Paris, Gallimard, 1976.

Stephen Motika, *Arrival and at Mono*, Brooklyn, Sona, 2007.

Nathanaël, *Touch to Affliction*, Toronto, Coach House, 2006 ; "Sostenuto" (inédit) ; "Vigilous, Reel : Desire (a)s accusation," San Francisco, Albion, 2010; "La dernière citadelle," in *Spirale*, 2010 ; "Du jamais vu," in *Spirale*, 2010; *Sisyphus, Outdone. Theatres of the Catastrophal*, Callicoon (NY), Nightboat, 2012.

Yuriy Norshteyn, *Hedgehog in the Fog*, 1975.

Anne Philippe, *L'éclat de la lumière, entretiens avec Marie-Hélène Vieira da Silva et Arpaud Szenes*, Paris, Gallimard, 1978.

Rainer Maria Rilke, *Duino Elegies*, tr. Will Crichton and Mary C. Crichton, København, Green Integer, 2003; *The Notebooks of Malte Laurids Brigge*, tr. Stephen Mitchell, New York, Vintage, 1982.

Jean Roudaut, *L'art de la conversation*, Ellipses, 2009.

Michel van Schendel, *Mille pas dans le jardin font aussi le tour du monde*, Montréal, l'Hexagone, 2005.

Leonard Schwartz, *The Sudden*, Tucson, Chax, 2009.

Franz Schürch, *Chaos = zéro mort, encore, 1,2,3...*, Montréal, Rodrigol, 2007.

Zafer Senocak, *Atlas of a Tropical Germany : Essays on Politics and Culture*, tr. L. Adelson, Lincoln (NE), Nebraska, 2000.

Brian Teare, *Sight Map*, Berkeley (CA), California, 2009; *The Room Where I was Born*, Madison (WI), University of Wisconsin, 2003.

John Tipton, *"hic domus incenditur,"* inédit, 2010.

Discord   Eugène Ionesco: Tout cela s'est desséché petit à petit. C'est devenu mince comme une feuille, mince et transparent comme une lame de verre très fine; transparent, puis ça s'est cassé sans bruit, ça a disparu.

André Malraux: N'oubliez pas que celui qui nous contemple, je veux dire l'histoire, qui nous juge et nous jugera, a besoin du courage qui gagne et pas de celui qui console.

Emmanuel Lévinas: C'est dans l'être même qui commence et non pas dans ses rapports avec sa cause que réside le paradoxe de l'être qui commence à être, c'est-à-dire l'impossibilité de dissocier en lui ce qui accepte le poids de ce poids lui-même.

Édouard Glissant: Car l'écriture, comme l'Un, est un manque consenti.

Glissant: La meute de moi taris se précipite sur ces morceaux de viande.

Roland Barthes: précisément ce compromis entre une liberté et un souvenir, (…) cette liberté souvenante qui n'est liberté que dans le geste du choix, mais déjà plus dans sa durée.

Georges Bataille: Je le savais déjà que l'intimité des choses est la mort.

Arthur Rimbaud: He's known all of us and has loved us all.

Edmond Jabès: Démente est la mer de ne pouvoir mourir d'une seule vague.

Jabès: Le désert n'a point de livre. / Le désert où notre impuissance nous refoule.

Albert Camus: je me trouve en face d'une métaphysique de la consolation.

Pierre-Alain Buhler: Que fais-tu quand la minuterie s'arrête? Je

Camus: témoignage obstiné d'une vie sans consolation

Nina Bouraoui: Nous dressons un mur, une prison dans une prison. // Nous renversons la ville.

Assia Djebar: Après tout, si j'avais été urbaniste, architecte ou sociologue de l'espace urbain, ç'aurait été sur les lieux mêmes de la déchéance qu'il aurait fallu habiter...

Guy Hocquenghem: Sa main ne répondait plus aux commandes du cerveau. C'était sa première mort.

Isaiah: CONSOLEZ, consolez mon peuple, dit votre Dieu. Parlez au coeur de Jérusalem, et criez-lui que son temps d'épreuve est fini, que son crime est expié, qu'elle a reçu de la main du Seigneur double peine pour toutes ses fautes.

Bernard-Marie Koltès: La fuite à cheval très loin dans la ville

Kateb Yacine: Un rêve dans un rêve, un monde dans un monde, un État dans l'État: telle sera, une fois le signal donné, notre insurrection générale.

Jean-Luc Nancy: La mise en branle du lieu est identiquement celle de l'instant présent.

Nancy: ce n'est pas en finissant, c'est en infinissant.

Le Corbusier: le cheval sans pattes; la chenille mécanique; du champ de bataille au champ de blé

André Malraux: ...l'Occident, que je concevais comme un pays dévoré par la géométrie.

Ilana Shmueli: ...lance sa haine sur toi.

Jacques Derrida: l'anastasis continue, fût-ce avec la rigueur de quelque cruauté, de consoler.

Paul de Man: Le mouvement de l'original est un déplacement, une errance, sorte d'exil permanent se l'on veut, sauf que ce n'est pas un exil, car il n'y a pas de patrie, rien dont on soit exilé.

Jean-Luc Nancy: Un qui vient à soi en s'entendant adresser la parole tout comme en s'entendant crier (répondre à l'autre? l'appeler?)

Catherine Mavrikakis: Elles se sont arraché les cheveux, crevé les yeux, en ouvrant une lettre.

Catherine Mavrikakis: Mais vous avez le pouvoir de nous consoler de ce que nous fûmes.

Yves Bonnefoy: Car il fallait des yeux pour les voir mais aussi des mains pour les prendre.

Claude Cahun: Écrivez-moi des lettres comme vous savez le faire: vivantes, émouvantes, l'illusion d'une presence.

Thierry Hentsch: Aucune catégorie jamais ne me contiendra.

Olivier Mannoni et Pierre Borassa: La langue de Beuys est tantôt abstraite, tantôt concrète. Elle est personelle, parfois à la limite de la compréhensibilité. Les traducteurs, confrontés à ce dilemme, se sont décidés pour l'intelligibilité.

Tahar Djaout: Si tu parles tu meurs, si tu ne parles pas tu meurs, alors parle et meurs.

Georges Bataille: sais-tu jusqu'à quel point l'homme est "toi-même"? imbécile? et nu?

Bernard-Marie Koltès: L'avantage provisoire du mot "frère" sur tout autre mot désignant ce qui lie quelqu'un à quelqu'un c'est qu'il est dépourvu de toute sentimentalité, de toute affectivité; ou, en tous les cas, on peut facilement l'en débarrasser. Il peut être dur, agressif, fatal, presque dit avec regret. Et puis il suggère l'irréversibilité et le sang (pas le sang des rois, des familllles ou des races, celui qui est tranquillement enfermé dans le corps et qui n'a pas plus de sens ni de couleur ni de prix que l'estomac ou la moelle épinière, mais celui qui sèche sur le trottoir.)

Deliberation   Jacques Derrida: Mais comme moi et moi nous mourrons, vous n'en doutez pas, il y a là une nécessité structurellement posthume de mon rapport—et du vôtre—à l'événement de ce texte qui ne s'arrive jamais.

Marguerite Duras: Ils ont dit que ce qu'ils cherchaient, c'était être eux-mêmes, et que j'y étais arrivé, moi, à être moi et que ce fait d'y arriver était un suicide, c'était un suicide de tous les autres possibles de soi.

Catherine Mavrikakis: Libre à nous de faire ce que nous voulons de nos personnages. Nous sommes tristes, immensément tristes, mais libres. Tu comprends ma fille ? Libres, même dans la violence et l'horreur qui s'abattent sur nous. Libres de donner à la mort radoteuse le sens qui nous convient.

Maurice Blanchot / Paul Celan: comme si avait déjà eu lieu la destruction de soi pour qu'autrui soit préservé ou pour que soit maintenu un signe porté par l'obscurité.

Pierre Schneider: La blessure faite au loin saigne tout près de nous.

Vieira da Silva: Quand vous peignez gris, vous avez toutes les couleurs.

Hélène Cixous: Lorsqu'on venait de mourir ma mort, la tienne, les jets de larmes bouillantes empêchaient que je visse vos visages.

Noëlle Renaude: …on décide de son désastre quand on est sur le plateau…

Hélène Cixous: Montaigne voulait mourir à cheval, merveilleuse mort sans toit.

Hervé Guibert: Comme la photographie peut n'être qu'un événement de lumière, sans sujet (et c'est le moment où elle est le plus photographie), j'aimerais un jour me lancer dans un récit qui ne serait qu'un événement d'écriture, sans histoire, et sans ennui, une véritable aventure.

Hervé Guibert: Sans lui, je n'écris pas, voilà la réalité, il écrit autant que moi en mettant sa langue dans ma bouche comme une irrigation brûlante qui devrait ne jamais cesser, et en la retirant, il est le coauteur absolu puisque l'écriture ne se fait que du manque de cette langue hors de ma bouche, de ce sexe hors de mes intestins, de cet éloignement intolérable du jumeau nécessaire.

Hervé Guibert: C'est vers la littérature que je veux aller, ou c'est vers la mort, ou c'est la même chose?

Marcel Proust: …libre comme dans un monde.

Hervé Guibert: L'expérience de la douleur est-elle préférable à l'anéantissement de l'expérience ?

Albert Camus: Tout est permis ne signifie pas que rien n'est défendu.

Jacques Derrida: …il t'aura fallu désemparer la mémoire, désarmer la culture, savoir oublier le savoir, incendier la bibliothèque des poétiques…

Bernard-Marie Koltès: Car tout homme ou animal redoute, à cette heure où l'homme marche à la même hauteur que l'animal et où tout animal marche à la même hauteur que tout homme, ce n'est pas la souffrance, car la souffrance se mesure, et la capacité d'infliger et de tolérer la souffrance se mesure ; ce qu'il redoute par-dessus tout, c'est l'étrangeté de la souffrance, et d'être amené à endurer une souffrance qui ne lui soit pas familière.

Émil Cioran: Une maladie n'est bien nôtre qu'à partir du moment où on nous en dit le nom, où on nous met la corde au cou…

Simone de Beauvoir: …la mort ne se pense pas.

Nina Bouraoui: Je cherche un corps qui consolera… La mort entre dans l'été.

Gaston Bachelard: Toujours, en nos rêveries, la maison est un grand berceau.

Imre Kertész: La dictature et le temps. La conception primitive de la vie et le temps. L'homme et le temps, non ; l'homme, essentiellement en tant que temps. Donc, l'homme n'est manifestement rien.

Imre Kertész: La liberté se mesure peut-être à la quantité et à la variété d'incognitos qu'on peut revêtir…

Claude Lanzmann: …toute mort 'naturelle' est d'abord mort violente.

Claude Lanzmann: Alors je suis peut-être mort car la chronologie de ma vie s'est complètement abolie, je pénètre dans ses circulaires spirales par mille chemins.

Mahmoud Darwish: Tant que je rêve c'est que je suis vivant. Les morts ne rêvent pas.

Claude Lanzmann: Car choisir c'est tuer. Ma mère était incapable de choisir, elle voulait tout. Je suis comme elle. J'ai pris pour sujet de diplôme d'études supérieures de philosophie: "Les possibles et les incompossibles dans la philosophie de Leibniz." Incompossible, cela veut dire qu'il y a des choses qui ne sont pas possibles ensemble, élire, l'une, c'est interdire à l'autre d'exister. Tout choix est un meurtre, on reconnaît, paraît-il, les chefs à leur capacité meurtrière, on les appelle des "décideurs", on les paie pour cela très cher. Ce n'est pas un hasard si Shoah dure neuf heures trente.

Anne Dufourmantelle: On a peur de tout ce qui signe notre aveu de dépendance, c'est-à-dire du sexe, de l'amour et de la pensée… qui sont probablement la même chose. On se voudrait libre et maître de soi, au moins un tout petit peu. Or le sexe comme la philosophie sont des expériences de chimie rigoureuses et fatales. Avec ce reste de silence autour que les mots de toute part environnent.

Roland Barthes: L'amoureux qui n'oublie pas quelquefois, meurt par excès, fatigue et tension de mémoire—

Jean-Luc Nancy: Je finit/s pare n'être plus qu'un fil ténu, de douleur en douleur et d'étrangeté en étrangeté.

Claude Cahun: Car déjà je traîne après moi trop de cadavres.

Jacques Lacan: Le désir s'ébauche dans la marge où la demande se déchire du besoin:

Marguerite Duras: On nous avait trompé sur l'âge de ce cheval.

Marguerite Duras: Je pourrais parler des heures de cette maison. Le jardin. Je connais tout. Je connais la place des anciennes portes. Tout. Les murs de l'étang. Toutes les plantes. La place de toutes les plantes. Même les plantes sauvages. Je connais la place. Tout.

Marguerite Duras: C'est au théâtre qu'à partir du manque, on donne tout à voir.

Marguerite Duras: Il y a pas de conflit. Ça se vit seul.

Duras: Il meurt comme un cheval, avec une force insoupçonnable.

Summation   Hervé Guibert: Il faudrait alors faire le silence, et que chacun s'efforce d'aller vers la violence de l'autre en dissipant la sienne.

André Malraux: En face de cette question, que m'importe ce qui n'importe qu'à moi?

Jean Genet: l'architecture du théâtre … doit être fixe, immobilisée, afin qu'on la reconnaisse responsable: elle sera jugée sur sa forme.

Édouard Glissant: Rien n'est vrai, tout est vivant.

Bernard-Marie Koltès: ...et jusque dans ton sommeil, je le jure, jusque dans ta mort, je te suivrai.

Marguerite Duras: Le désir est mort, tué par une image.

André Gorz: Il faut accepter d'être fini: d'être ici et nulle part ailleurs, de faire ça et pas autre chose, maintenant et non jamais ou toujours [...] d'avoir cette vie seulement.

Pippo Delbono : Tu danses parce que tu es conscient de la mort.

Gorz: Kafka: Mon amour de toi ne s'aime pas.

Jean-François Lyotard: Le récit de la fin d'un temps se raconte dans un nouveau temps qui conserve cette fin et, par là même, se présente comme un début.

Malraux: ...cet inoubli de l'oubli qui n'est pas la mémoire.

Hervé Guibert: ...j'ai besoin de catastrophes, de coups de theatre...

Nancy: l'anéantissement anéanti, la fin ... privée d'elle-même

Lyotard: bouche[s] blessée[s] qui bée[nt] sur le vide

René Char: Que fera-t-on de nous, après?

Malraux: Nous sommes habités par des monstres banals. // Aucune religion, aucune expérience ne nous a dit que l'épouvante est en nous. (...) Le monstre a occupé mes décombres, puis ma conscience qui se perdait dans le sommeil; enfin, ce chemin s'est dissipé—mais je l'avais reconnu, je le reconnaîtrai, comme ces rêves où l'on pense; j'ai déjà rêvé cela.

Pierre Fédida: Mais où commence la fin de la vie? Non pas quand, mais où?

Franz Schürch: Tous étranglés parce que le feu vous mérite

Cioran: Se détruit quiconque, répondant à sa vocation et l'accomplissant, s'agite à l'intérieur de l'histoire;

Cioran: On périt toujours par le moi qu'on assume: porter un nom c'est revendiquer un mode exact d'effondrement.

Cioran: Point d'œuvre qui ne se retourne contre son auteur, le poème écrasera le poète, le système le philosophe, l'événement l'homme d'action.

Jacques Derrida: Toi, faut que ce soit toi.

Christophe Donner: Des textes qui forment enfin un objet. On les croit tangibles. Une œuvre endure. L'écrivain n'est pas un artiste à cause de ça. La matière n'est pas de son ressort. Il la poursuit. C'est risible. Il doit s'y faire. Ce n'est pas un écrivain qui a inventé l'écriture.

Stig Dagerman: Car si ce désir n'existe pas, qu'est-ce qui peut alors exister?

Maurice Blanchot: Et pourtant, toujours, nous nous choisissons un compagnon: non pour nous, mais pour quelque chose en nous, hors de nous, qui a besoin que nous manquions à nous-mêmes pour passer la ligne que nous n'atteindrons pas.

Roland Castro: Moi qui suis né exterminable, c'est pour ça que je suis en vie.

Marguerite Duras: Ni quels sont les lieux, les scènes, les capitales, les continents où tu as crié la passion des amants.

Duras: Si moi je mourais, tout le monde mourrait, alors… ça n'existe pas…

Brigitte Salino: On ne peut pas aimer le théâtre si on n'aime pas l'ennui.

Duras: , la douleur se propose comme une solution à la douleur, comme un deuxième amour.

Danielle Collobert: Non ça n'est pas fini. Il faut entendre encore, entendre la voix, les questions, s'encourager, se protéger, aussi se débattre pour aller jusqu'au bout, avec cette immense lâcheté de préférer les mots, leur édifice, au petit geste, inconcevable, que je n'arrive pas encore à faire.

Marguerite Duras: Si je veux on me prend pour un enfant de quarante ans de philosophie.

André Malraux: Le jour anniversaire de ma quarantième année, lorsque je passais clandestinement la ligne de démarcation avec le chat noir, j'aurais voulu être né la veille.

In the time between speaking, at a closed window, and with seemingly no door, there occurred an intensification of meaning that could only result in the abolishment of further memory. In the way of an evacuation. In the way C. would say to me over the course of the period of the carnets that I was the evacuation channel of a particular experience. A name with no residue, that could only be residual, and in this sense, could signify, most immediately, a repository of numerous, contradictory discrepancies. Between a stack of paintings stored in a basement that didn't flood when Chicago's streets were mired in shit and a bathtub on the north side that didn't contain my corpse. It was February. These are details, they are of no interest, and by calling attention to them, they become falsifications not only of themselves but of the uses I might make of them, particularly in light of their contrived chronology. Nonetheless, what matters to me here is the exact inversion which is being proposed by these two instances, namely the excess such as the city could not contain, set against the empty bathtub. There is in French no adequate word to translate the English word vacuum. A dictionary will indicate *le vide*, but *le vide* is as much a vacuum as it is a void or emptiness, and out of this sometimes welcome ambiguity, there is the loss of a particular specificity, and with it, a particular experience of isolation.

In 2011, I returned to France after having not set foot there for twenty-one years. It is imaginable that one could suspend one's memory over such a period of time; also, that one could die of it. And that this particular death might occur first inside one's mouth, since there is so much of one that dies in the mouth, beginning perhaps with one's name. If for twenty-one years this refusal oriented me, in language, in emotion, and in my sense of history or desire, its sublimation has functioned as much as an impetus as a debilitation. So why expose it in this light, if not to make material to myself what might be a necessary latency for the sake of survival. R. says survival is bullshit. She is as emphatic as the bird that crashes against the glass made by humans. Everything shatters, and if the lure of vitality is subsumed into an artifice of over-living, then what right have we to admire the dance of grebes or the luminosity of spiders? I am the first to blame. Myself and then everyone. For the murder of the species. First we murder ourselves. Then the world we belong to. Six days and a scarred moon over the tin roofs of Avenue de Saxe in a maid's room with a seatless toilet on the landing.

There is no telling what part of Duras's *The War* is fabrication, and what exactly it is that she is putting on trial, and thereby perhaps exonerating. But there is this which is to be taken from it: that *The War* itself attempts to correct or perhaps apologize for something the French title *La douleur* invites—and that is the ache of the very history she is recording. Memory invites every kind of despondency. If, *a posteriori*, I have extended the time of the prior carnets to include the pages fallen from another book, it is to make public, first to myself, the exclusion of certain histories that can only be consummated on the public square, in which I, the writer, become the reader I must assassinate.

The *Untendered Pages* that follow, fell between the bathtub and the lake, and if I didn't burn them, or drown them, it must be that something in me awoke to their necessity.

—Nathanaël
Chicago, 2014

UNTENDERED
PAGES
(2011)

Or, *tout homme*, fortuitement ou non, peut être pendu. Cette égalité est intolérable.

—*René Char*

Still, *every man*, fortuitously or not, can be hanged. This equality is intolerable.

—*René Char*

Sleep. I know it can wait, but I wanted to tell you that I followed your advice last night when I couldn't sleep, I boiled some water, I turned on the little light, I read several pages more from the Austrian philosopher's biography. I'm not sure I was able to still the litanies inside, nor the anguish of 'lost sleep,' but I was relieved by the presence of your voice which supplanted mine sometimes. I wrote nothing, as I can sometimes be immobilized by writing, which is terrible for a person whose life is comprised almost exclusively of that.

...

I would limit myself to these words of Kafka's : *It was as if the shame of it would outlive him*.

...

The most exact suicide note : Stig Dagerman's.

...

Does a suicide present itself as inevitable once it has been consigned to language ? Collobert, for example. Pizarnik.

...

By changing the space occupied by my name in the alphabet, have I thwarted—or precipitated—mine ?

...

It isn't that I want it, but that it wants me.

...

And I was able to believe in both will and want. Now the simple fact of saying I seems to want to exclude the dilemma in favour of an end.

...

For nothing, I could—

...

The burden of a name is too great?

...

I was wrong to have wanted it. To have imagined any of it otherwise.

...

Now I have managed even to destroy the space of the library.

...

The entire logic of my existence will have been in that direction.

...

I show the photograph of me. It is my first, and my last, infidelity.

...

You must have anticipated everything. That by reinserting it in the otherwise-world, it should lose its precise meaning. It should cease to exist such as it is. Such as it did exist. I see now that there was no fire. Nothing lit. Other than the desire for this thing, which invented it in the place of that nothing. No one saw it coming.

...

I will be met at the airport. I will follow the road to the city. A city which is my underside, a sort of catacomb, I suppose, after all this time, but perhaps the glimmer also of a misplaced vital thing.

...

Today I am all of my forty years, twice that, and one way or another, at this precise moment, the violent current that carries me is far from me and I have no desire to follow it, and if on the one hand I am horrified, on the other I am riveted to this instant, and it is hard for me to imagine another age.

...

But the days are poorly indicated, because it is in fact the second half of Sunday, the moon at the window.

...

A city among cities. A language among languages.

...

A headline of *Courrier international* : L'Occident, est-il fini ?

...

It is impossible for me to narrate this voyage. But I find that nothing is such as I had imagined it. That my memory is more vigilant than I had thought, that my fear shows itself where I least expect it, and the city folds into me at another rhythm altogether. In sum, I could say of here that it is still me ; or rather, that it is me in spite of the city.

...

Whatever force is in me, exceeds me : I can be grateful for that.

...

Tomorrow I shall take the train. I am avoiding being overly enthusiastic, and preventing myself as well from giving myself over to the sadness that is sometimes intent upon submerging me.

...

It is after midnight, I'm under the blue sheets in a bed set upon the floor, some six or seven hours ahead of you. This is the fourth day, the fifth day of travel given that I left at noon.

...

On the table, an orange tile, a cast iron teapot, a purple orchid and a ball of yarn, tears that won't hold still.

...

I am standing in front of you, in front of all of this. And I am afraid of being even more of a disappointment, to myself and to the friendships which hold me. If I think that I am already dead, what can go wrong ? I hope to die dignified and indignant, and more than anything, *in love*—

...

It's clear that the armature of this voyage is friendship.

...

The crêperie, and the weather cooled, the wind rose, and we had tea later at the apartment. They went to see a film and I excused myself, returned at around 10 pm by the same Métro, and reassured of nothing, but happy for the time spent together.

...

Fleeting city.

...

I recognize nothing.

...

I slept on the floor in the office.

...

The dreams before waking depleted me of everything. Many incidents, places and people. You were there. We were walking, there was the lagoon, I couldn't cross it. You were there and you weren't, coming, going, and I couldn't leave the square. J and J were there as well at another moment in addition to someone I hadn't thought of in over thirty years, a picnic table in another square, the grocery was closed, I had wanted to buy flowers. In a cellar, J found a small bouquet of my favourite flowers ; take them, she said ; which we did in fact do and they were stolen. My mother appeared and wouldn't stop touching me.

...

But in the most wrenching dream, I was walking naked in an old city, I was walking, I think, toward the butte, cobbles, etc. There was a man (a stranger in the dream and in my memory) and he wouldn't stop taking my photograph ; maliciously ; I tried to take his camera from him, but couldn't. This carried on endlessly and I wasn't able to cover myself, even when I was inside again (a place crammed full of people), I couldn't escape, and whatever I did, to return toward the place I had left, I had to pass in front of him. It's almost futile to try to interpret this too carefully since the meaning is more or less explicit. But it's perhaps reason enough to be suspicious of the apparent exegetical banality. Well, it was a pleasure to meet you and to walk together a while. The rest seems to be a mixture of times and disturbances which are so obvious as to be of no interest at present.

...

The city carries on its elusive game of non-memory smothered by the sense of an inarticulable recognition.

...

I cannot dispute this notice, *epic*, as much as my literary good sense ought to. This whole situation is outside of every range of reference.

...

The books are not me. They are what cannot subsist in

me, what in me could not subsist without the necessary evacuations. It's a form of torture to be held to them, to have them shoved back into me.

...

Plant the poppies if you must, but plant them with the kale and the beets, and admire them for their livid beauty.

...

Since 4:30, the dark roads, the controls and my lunch has been duly searched. The airport offers the one advantage of being a non-place. I think I can wish you good-night from here this dark morning, as it must be close to time.

...

A friend writes to tell me she is going to take an apartment on the seventeenth floor of a building. My first thought is that she is going to jump. My hands are desperate before this unsaid intention.

...

I haven't yet read Walt Whitman. M. threatens to read him to me if I don't keep my word. I imagined you in unison, a sort of Whitmaniacal seduction—accented, of course—and it gave me pleasure, even if fleeting.

...

Here the days since the naturalisation are an accumulation of devastations. As though someone had ripped off the skin of last summer and driven me into an identical intranquillity. The same goring accusations. Almost a week. A sleep ever more ravaged by dreams, and palpitating, and eroded wakings. I am more and more stupid. Sleeping and crying and sleeping because of crying and waking crying from sleep. I am laughing. What else can I do? Laughter and the Solomon's Seal planted on the back balcony and the lavender and Thunbergia that you will see. The city is replete with this vivid summer, leaving the indolence of spring.

...

Dead is dead.

...

And yet the vital goad urges us deeper into the fire as it burns.

...

I am in a good mood, or else in that light, sometimes delirious mood that precedes a collapse. I will have spent the entire day in my bed, thinking of nothing. I read three pages of a book and that is all. Now I am writing you.

...

One says, I think, of the hours that they are hollow. Of the cheeks as well. And hunger.

...

One says that one digs one's hole. Does one dig sometimes one's bed? One's idiocy?

...

We will have tea one day, that will be all. But that very tea makes me want to split my head open against the wall.

...

Tomorrow, I'm cancelling the telephone. It was either that or the apartment.

...

I'm clearing surfaces.

...

The Stars-of-Bethlehem are throwing their colour on the walls, into the eyes of the cats.

...

(Bis): Awake since 4:30, I can't make up my mind. Several hours lost to thinking about narrative, the limits imposed by narrative. Wonder, nonetheless, whether this distrust of narrative will succeed in extracting me from it, or whether, by rejecting it, I am in fact prolonging what cannot disappear so long as it will not have taken form, even destroyed.

...

Last weekend's anemones are tinted pink now, deeply deployed; in the night, it's as though they'd torn their hair out. Onto them, I project my insomnias.

...

Do you think it possible for song to exist away from the shame of being human?

...

It's that I drew the curtains against the day.

...

Do you know, there are mechanisms that set off, and we aren't stupid, we watch them do their thing, the total disintegration of the self, still we tell ourselves that we are watching them so how are we to stop them and whence the certainty that *there is not* hasn't confiscated the sheets?

...

Slowly I cut the current. I close the curtains. I lie down on my face. Inside, it spills, the circuits trip effortlessly. Just like that.

...

So I go out and I walk. Someone opens a door and I almost fall under the shock of that movement. So I go in quickly and it screams inside. The same litanies, the same invectives, the same you not.

...

Must one leave quickly, on the plumes of one's capsize?

...

Yes, *loriot*.
Yes, *merlebleu*.
Yes, *moineau*.
Grive is the most beautiful of words; thank you.

...

The eye of the sky opens this morning onto you from this Chicago, the geese, the warmth of the voices tendered by the throats that proffer them.

...

I would like for someone to explain to me this mechanism of successful willed amnesia coupled with the activation of a place in the body as though it remembered everything.

...

This morning I opened the windows for the first time since winter.

...

I am starting to understand that through a tree, too, one can embrace a person.

...

Thank you for tearing a lost voice on the letter you are making me.

...

I imagine a city covered in anemones. Then covered in enemies. And the part of my mind that imagines the city faints and collapses on the floor of a country house abandoned amid howling winds that shatter the windows.

...

I will open my mouth and others will scream. I will be locked up in the Bastille without food or light and my love of anemones will be denounced.

...

This morning I finally found a copy of Quartet no. 8, Opus 110, and set about settling the score, the second movement—*allegro molto.* For hours I remained seated before the two-minute and thirty-eight-second segment, performed by the

Emerson Quartet, my eye trained on the musical text—the equivalent of a dozen sheets or so. With each reading, I found myself more and more illiterate. The whole notes could just as easily have been quarter notes, and the quarter notes thirty-seconds. I was dizzy with it, more and more dizzy, until after several dozen attempts, I was able, if only fleetingly, to coordinate the passage I was reading with the one I was listening to. Having arrived there, I was so ravaged by the music—this piece, as you know, was written by Shostakovitch after having visited Dresden, and dedicated to "the memory of the victims of fascism and war"—that the pleasure, however fleeting, of having decoded the score doubled by the exhaustion occasioned by such a labour near threw me to the floor: I cried.

I started again, and it was just as futile; the music had left me, or my ability to read. And I continued to resort to more and more rudimentary strategies, counting bars with my finger and identifying the most rudimentary passages—reading the pauses in order to compensate for my inability to follow the rapid execution—I was at the antipodes of your *sostenuto*. Shostakovitch cried when he wrote this piece, and me, I cried out of sheer labour, invaded by a regret (or a question) tied to musical abandon. On New Year's Eve, a poet spoke to me of his opera lessons when he was a young man: his teacher required him to lie on the floor on his back and sing; he continued like this for days and weeks, months no doubt, before being invited to stand.

...

The unwritten part of this letter recounts to you in inopportune detail the astonishing dispatch of memories from too long ago. I leave them be. Suffice it to say that the Lyon is at my door.

...

The weeks, the days, have become dangerous, the body capitulates to its most desperate damagings, and from week to week it worsens in ways unheard of, though with moments of reprieve and an intensity also which belies the kinds of endings I saw myself soliciting. Complicated messagings against a self in a world, a demented language that disallows an I and mutilated speaking, a pain at the throat, weeks now, the muteness, the strain. My back to the wall of a small garage, my mouth stuffed full of crematorium, convinced of the invincibility of my failure, replete with a kind of madness overwritten by forms of functionality that make the madness more maddening, and sleep impossible. Days and weeks of insomnia, some three or four hours at most, the days shot through with adrenaline, eyes too wide and my fists bruising my chest in my thwarted sleep from dream to undreamt dream of violence unto violence, the seams of me bursting against the imminence of a country and the conviction that it will kill me.

...

Yesterday I spoke your name, and I saw that you weren't there.

...

I walked and I walked, I wanted to gather evidence in favour of a life that wouldn't require that writing always be bartered against living, and for which living wasn't always a postponement provoked by writing. And I asked myself whether it was even true, or whether I was capable, once more, of prolonging this justification.

...

What astonishes me : when you say *grive* to me or else *laisse*, I have a profound sense of the attachment of these words to specific places, to lives, whereas me, when I say *mer* or else *moineau*, the words are empty, of sense perhaps— of sensation.

...

Monday, now. I am able once more to swallow my saliva without swallowing my throat with it.

...

Every day my body catches fire. Today is no exception. Sun, nonetheless. I will walk in the cemetery under a sun that gouges the eyes.

...

The Lyon is dead. At the Paris florists, no anemones. I thought of your descents.

...

The silence is prolonged. I don't yet dare give you my voice.

...

After you left, I walked to the edge of the water with the many sadnesses, and this which is in my body now. It isn't a fear but a tragic thing, perhaps, the way the tragic can belong to the real (now it is Ionesco, thinking in me).

...

It is you who are the angel. Any, more ?

...

"I left." Me too, my friend.

...

There were so many letters inside, from that door, 727, to this one, 1448.

...

Slow waking in the early part of the day, a tea near a window looking out at a cemetery. The gate is open and the geese are silent and the people walk past in their day and I wonder how many of them have just come away from a body, have come out of a bed, facing another way.

...

Extended past touch, unsleeping.

...

This is what I think this morning, in the dim, forensic light. Past the determination of a face, the inhabited present, the trees along the lake marking your eyes, a disconcerting cinema and detached from the movement of the car, the facture of the road, I forget the hospital and the midnight emergencies, the shrill mind, the shrieking, it all unravels in favour of a moment unfurled toward other wheres.

...

A house with fragile walls, and the heart. The hand on a skin, the hollow of a clavicle, a patch of hair, my hand and then the rest of me.

...

When you write "affirmation," I read "infirmity".

...

After having poured scalding water on my left hand the other day, without somehow having burned it, this morning, slicing a vegetable, I managed to insert the blade into the index of my left hand, beneath the cuticle and towards the knuckle, such that it is a perfect wound, deeply bruised, and barely visible.

...

I am listening near you. That voice of twenty years ago.

...

Yesterday I walked, we walked, near the lake, rain and wind, the heart lit.

...

Monday: I am Americanizing. Every night I dream of the death of my sister, it must be because of that, that definitive rupture of the border.

...

But I too, like you, I could say of these days: nothing. Nothing.

The only anemone: purple, deployed, and the colour of which tears on its own colour, sensual, with a dark, aching, centre.

By The Same [sic] Author

ISBN 978–1–937658–38–0

Aspects of *The Middle Notebookes* and *Untendered Pages*
were present in various stages of undress in the pages of
Chicago Review, *CLOCK*, *Mandorla*, *Poetry Northwest*,
Staging Ground, *TriQuarterly*, *Vanitas*, *Very Small Kitchen*
and *VOLT*. With due gratitude to the hospitable
editors thereof.

Design and typesetting
Mark Addison Smith

Images by Nathanaël
Cover: *Pluies 02* (2010)
P. 423: *Anemone* (2011)

Distributed by
University Press of New England
One Court Street
Lebanon, NH 03766
www.upne.com

Nightboat Books
New York
www.nightboat.org

About Nightboat Books

Nightboat Books, a nonprofit organization, seeks to develop audiences for writers whose work resists convention and transcends boundaries. We publish books rich with poignancy, intelligence, and risk. Please visit nightboat.org to learn more about us and how you can support our future publications.

The following individuals have supported the publication of this book. We thank them for their generosity and commitment to the mission of Nightboat Books:

Elizabeth Motika
Benjamin Taylor

In addition, this book has been made possible, in part, by grants from the National Endowment for the Arts and the New York State Council on the Arts Literature Program.